FIGHT FOR YOUR RIGHTS

A Federal Employee's Guide
to the EEO Process

by

Michael J. Snider, Esq.
Morris E. Fischer, Esq.

FIGHT FOR YOUR RIGHTS
Copyright © 2006
Michael J. Snider, Esq.
Morris E. Fischer, Esq.

International Standard Book Number:　　　0-9723136-1-3

Printed in the United States of America.

THIS PUBLICATION IS DESIGNED TO PROVIDE ACCURATE AND AUTHORITATIVE INFORMATION WITH REGARD TO THE SUBJECT MATTER COVERED. IT IS DISTRIBUTED WITH THE UNDERSTANDING THAT THE PUBLISHER IS NOT ENGAGED IN RENDERING LEGAL OR OTHER PROFESSIONAL ADVICE BY THIS PUBLICATION. IF LEGAL ADVICE OR OTHER EXPERT ADVICE IS REQUIRED, THE SERVICES OF A COMPETENT PROFESSIONAL PERSON SHOULD BE SOUGHT.

Dedications

To my dear wife, Ruth.

To Mom, Dad, Aba, Ima, Savta, Sara Tova, Avi, Aron Dovid, Akiva, and Shlomo Yeshaya.

Thanks to Sean, Don, and Regina.

Thanks to the Team.

In memory of Saba, R' Yuda Tzvi ben HaRav Akiva ZTZ"L, who always fought for Justice.

Table of Contents

Introduction

The federal government is the nation's single largest employer with more than 2.4 million employees. In addition, not only is the federal government the largest employer in the country, but it's also one of the most diverse. The federal government employs people of every race, creed and color. Even more, it claims to be committed to providing equal employment opportunity to all Americans. In fact, the federal government has gone so far as to make this policy the law of the land.

"It is the policy of the Government of the United States to provide equal opportunity in employment for all persons, to prohibit discrimination in employment because of race, color, religion, sex, national origin, age or handicap and to promote the full realization of equal employment opportunity through a continuing affirmative program in each agency."

Yet, despite the federal government's admirable efforts in this regard, the federal workplace is by no means free from all forms of discrimination. After all, the federal government is run by people – people who bring their own biases and prejudices to the job. As a result, each year, incidents of discrimination arise in relation to promotions, pay raises, training opportunities, failures to accommodate and the creation of hostile work environments.

Fortunately, the victims of discrimination aren't powerless to assert their rights to equal employment opportunity. The federal government has established an elaborate administrative EEO process to handle claims of discrimination. This process is available to the following federal civilian employees working within the U.S.:

- All non-uniformed employees of military departments, such as the Department of Defense;

- All employees of executive agencies, such as the Department of Homeland Security, U.S. Treasury, and Secret Service;

- All employees of the U.S. Postal Service, the Postal Rate Commission, the Tennessee Valley Authority, the National Oceanic and Atmospheric Administration Commissioned Corps, the

Government Printing Office, and the Smithsonian Institution; and

- All employees of the judicial branch who have positions in the competitive service.

Each year, tens of thousands of federal workers utilize this system. For example, in 2003, there were 45,030 instances of discrimination reported to EEO offices in federal executive agencies, 17,019 of which resulted in formal EEO complaints being filed. In all, federal workers received millions of dollars in benefits to compensate for discrimination faced on the job.

Therefore, if you've been the victim of a discriminatory practice, you shouldn't feel hesitant about asserting your rights under this system. After all, that's what it's here for – to ensure that the federal government lives up to its stated policy of providing equal employment opportunity for all.

Of course, nothing in life is easy. To successfully file and prosecute a complaint under EEO regulations will require an intimate understanding of the rules in place. In this book, we provide you with just that. The purpose of this book is to explain the process and give you the tools you need to win your discrimination claim, or to represent others in their complaints.

If you're currently involved in the EEO process or even just thinking about filing, the information contained in these pages is crucial to helping you navigate the maze of EEO regulations. In fact, this is true even if you ultimately decide to hire an attorney to fight on your behalf. To resolve the dispute in your favor, your attorney is going to need a lot of help from you. Therefore, the more you understand about the process, the better you can equip your attorney to make the best possible case on your behalf. And, of course, if you choose to go it alone, you'll need every tip and technique at your disposal.

For this reason, this book is different from many books that simply discuss the legal process in broad strokes. Our goal in writing this book is to prepare you to actually take your case from the pre-complaint stage through the formal complaint and to the ultimate hearing before an administrative judge. To accomplish this task, you're going to need to know not only the theory but the actual practice of making your case. Therefore, this book not only contains a detailed explanation of the rules and regulations, but also many sample documents and forms so that you can see just how the process works. Copies of all referenced forms and document samples are included, and are available for download from our website as well.

Our sincere hope is that your investment of time and energy in reading this book will pay enormous dividends in equipping you to present the strongest possible case. Of course, we can't promise that you will be ultimately successful. Yet, we can promise to provide you with the very best information we've learned from the hundreds of cases we've dealt with in this area.

As a federal employee, you have the *right* to be free from discrimination on the basis of race, color, religion, gender, national origin, age or handicap. Working in an environment free from arbitrary discrimination isn't a privilege; it's a right. Yet, like all rights, this right must be fought for from time to time. In this book, we will teach you how to do just that. We thank you and wish you the best of luck.

Michael J. Snider, Esq.

Morris E. Fischer, Esq.

Chapter 1
Unlawful Discrimination

Before getting into the nuts and bolts of making your case in a complaint and at a hearing, it's important to take a moment to explain the legal rules regarding federal workplace discrimination claims. As you can imagine, federal employment discrimination statutes and EEOC regulations don't prohibit *all* forms of discrimination. For obvious reasons, federal employers can make differentiations between employees on the basis of skills, education, work performance and the like. These are all lawful types of discrimination. What federal law prohibits is "unlawful discrimination."

Therefore, it's important to spend a little time familiarizing yourself with the specifics of what constitutes unlawful discrimination under federal law. Of course, we realize that you're probably already somewhat familiar with your rights in this area. From our experience, we've learned that federal employees, in contrast to their private sector counterparts, are often more educated about their rights in the workplace. Nevertheless, we still believe it's helpful to review the legal bases of unlawful discrimination claims.

This is true even if you're already involved in the EEOC process and have been scheduled for a hearing. Your ultimate success in this battle is going to come down to how well you establish your case from a legal standpoint. You may have been subjected to treatment that was unfair, insensitive or just plain rude at the hands of your employer. Yet, an EEO Administrative Judge won't be able to rule in your favor (no matter how much he or she might like to) unless you make a clear and convincing *legal* argument that you've been the victim of unlawful discrimination.

The information in these next few chapters will help you to do just that, by explaining the specific legal basis for each form of unlawful discrimination. In fact, in reading through these chapters, you may uncover additional bases for your claim of discrimination before the EEOC that you may not have realized would apply. In later chapters, we'll explain how to amend your complaint, if necessary, to make your case the strongest possible case it can be.

Legal Bases for Discrimination Actions

As we discussed earlier, federal statutes prohibit discrimination based on race, color, religion, gender, national origin, age or handicap. However, to file a Complaint with the EEO office at your agency and to pursue your claim with the EEOC, you must have a claim for discrimination that is based directly upon one or more of four federal statutes that prohibit discrimination. They are:

- Title VII of the Civil Rights Act of 1964 (discrimination on the basis of race, color, religion, gender or national origin);

- The Age Discrimination in Employment Act of 1967 (discrimination on the basis of age);

- The Rehabilitation Act of 1973 (discrimination on the basis of disability); and

- The Equal Pay Act of 1963 (wage-based discrimination on the basis of gender).

As you may have noticed, none of these acts prohibit discrimination on the basis of sexual orientation, parental or marital status, veteran's status or political affiliation. Of course, this is not to say these types of discrimination are legal. Several states have laws prohibiting these forms of discrimination (although state discrimination law doesn't apply to federal employees). However, the federal employee EEO process isn't available for these types of claims. That being said, another forum may be available to you if you've been affected by discrimination on these other grounds, such as the Merit Systems Protection Board (www.mspb.gov) or the Office of Special Counsel (www.osc.gov). Therefore, if you've been the victim of one of these forms of discrimination, we recommend that you consult with a competent attorney to explore your rights in those areas.

A "Tangible" Employment Action

In addition to establishing unlawful discrimination, in most cases, you must also establish that the discrimination resulted in a "tangible" employment action. In other words, you must show that you lost something of tangible value due to being the victim of discrimination. In other words, the unlawful discrimination must usually have resulted in a tangible loss to the victim. And by "tangible," we mean something that an administrative judge or court can measure.

For instance, if the unlawful discrimination simply results in you feeling isolated or lonely in the workplace, that probably isn't enough to justify your EEO claim. The unlawful discrimination must generally have some measurable impact, such as a monetary loss from being unlawfully terminated or demoted. Of course, when the loss is monetary, it's very easy to quantify and thus, normally falls within the definition of a "tangible employment action."

In other cases, it isn't as easy to determine whether you suffered a tangible employment action. For example, let's suppose that you've been wrongly denied training opportunities or have been given a faulty evaluation. Let's further suppose that neither of these situations resulted in your termination or demotion. In that case, in order to have a valid EEO claim, you will need to *specifically* demonstrate how these actions could have long-term tangible effects on your career. This may require you to present expert testimony from a classification expert or specialist to support your claim that the loss of training opportunities or a faulty performance review would be viewed by management as a serious strike against you in a future promotion decision.

Finally, for these purposes, denial of accommodation (religious or disability) is usually a tangible employment action.

Hostile Work Environment

A major exception to the "tangible" employment action requirement is the situation where unlawful discrimination results in a "hostile work environment." The mere existence of a hostile work environment is a valid basis for an EEO claim in and of itself.

Like the name implies, a hostile work environment claim involves allegations that the workplace environment has become hostile to the employee as a result of that employee's race, gender, religion, etc. This is true whether the hostility was instigated by a manager, a co-worker or even a subordinate. Unless agency management takes *immediate* and appropriate action to put a stop to the offensive behavior, the employee could have a valid hostile work environment claim.

Hostile environment claims usually rise or fall on whether the harassment was "severe or pervasive." Obviously, these are rather subjective terms. We will try to help you further understand and support a case under these two (separate) criteria. Note that you only have to prove that the harassment was severe *or* pervasive – not both.

Very often, the issue in these cases is whether the conduct in question was sufficiently offensive to constitute a hostile work environment. As you can imagine, every case is different and therefore, creating a bright line test for harassment cases is next to impossible. However, as a general rule, workplace conduct will be considered to reach the level of hostile work environment when either: (1) it reaches the level of being outrageous; or (2) it is repeated on a regular and continuous basis. In other words, if it is "severe" or "pervasive."

For example, the victim of sexual assault on the job may have a very strong claim to a hostile work environment because the conduct in such cases is unquestionably outrageous. On the other hand, an employee who overhears a co-worker telling a sexually-explicit or racist joke may not have such a sure-fire claim for harassment, unless this incident is part of a larger pattern of harassment or occurs on a fairly regular basis. As a general rule, the more outrageous the conduct, the less often it need be repeated; and vice versa.

In order to prevail in a hostile environment claim, you need to show that the hostility was because of a protected basis (i.e., religion, race, gender, or national origin). Because there are no compensatory damages in age discrimination cases, it is not clear that a hostile work environment claim can effectively be based on age. In other words, without a loss in pay or usage of leave, an age-based hostile work environment claim is not likely to provide much in the way of damages.

You also will need to show some basis upon which to impute liability to the agency. If the harassment is by a supervisor, the agency may be held automatically vicariously liable. On the other hand, if the harassment is by a co-worker or non-supervisor, you must first complain to the agency and then to the agency must fail to act in a timely and appropriate manner before you have a case.

A large number of hostile work environment claims fail because the employee failed to complain about the situation. As we've said, your manager or supervisor or someone in charge (i.e., the "agency" management) must be on actual notice that you are suffering from a hostile work environment due to discrimination. In fact, in many cases, it isn't until you complain about the environment (and your manager fails to take action to stop it) that you even become a victim of a hostile work environment from a *legal* standpoint.

Please note that we aren't talking here about causes of action you might have against the harasser or attacker personally. However, in an EEO complaint, you are technically bringing an action against the head of the agency. As a result, the agency must have some notice of the objectionable behavior.

For obvious reasons, the best form of notice to provide your manager is a written record of complaint. After all, when court proceedings roll around, you will be taken seriously if you can produce, say, a certified letter to your manager complaining specifically about a hostile work environment based upon an illegal factor like race. This kind of evidence will certainly be far more persuasive than generalized and unsubstantiated testimony that you verbally mentioned to your supervisor that you were unhappy because of the environment.

Most hostile work environment cases involve claims of emotional stress and physical signs of depression, such as weight gain and insomnia. In these cases, agencies, administrative judges, and courts can award monetary damages based on those factors rather than merely tangible employment-related losses suffered by the victim of unlawful discrimination.

In the next four chapters, we will discuss the specifics of what's entailed in making a claim of unlawful discrimination under each of the four federal statutes mentioned above.

Chapter 2

Title VII

Title VII makes it unlawful for employers to refuse to hire or promote an individual based on his or her race, color, religion, gender or national origin. Likewise, it's unlawful to fire an employee or base his or her compensation or other terms and conditions of employment on these factors. Employers may not deprive an individual of employment opportunities, such as receiving additional training opportunities, on a prohibited basis. Finally, retaliation for filing a complaint or protesting discrimination is illegal as well.

Proof of discrimination takes one of three methods. Discrimination can be proven by direct evidence of discrimination (e.g., "I can't hire you for this job. You're a woman."), indirect evidence of discrimination (e.g., documentation illustrating that the complainant has been dealt with more harshly than persons of another race in similar situation) and disparate impact (e.g., only persons of one religion have been promoted to managerial positions in a certain department over the last ten years).

Race, Color or National Origin

Discrimination on the basis of race, color or national origin is perhaps the classic form of discrimination. Most commonly, it occurs when a manager refuses to hire someone just because they are of a particular race or nationality. In these cases, the manager may base his or her decision on the biased thought that "there are already enough black faces around here," "we can't hire a white person because our minority numbers are down" or "federal jobs should go to *real* Americans; not people from south of the border."

In other cases, the discrimination occurs *after* the individual is hired and results in his or her termination or denial of a promotion. Here the manager may base his or her actions on mistaken premises, such as "Asians are simply not assertive enough to be managers" or "Native Americans are just plain lazy."

Of course, these types of thoughts are rarely voiced out loud; at least, not to the victims of discrimination. In some cases, the real reason behind a termination or a refusal to hire only becomes known when the manager's close friends and confidants within the organization are interviewed. And even then, it's possible that the manager has never articulated these sentiments. In fact, the manager may not even be consciously aware that he or she subscribes to them.

For this reason, it's necessary in some cases to prove discrimination by presenting evidence that the manager treated the complainant differently than workers of different races. For example, we had a minority client who had been fired from her position. The given reason for the termination was "performance deficiencies." At the administrative hearing, we were able to demonstrate that our client's deficiencies were normal work problems and that non-minority employees had the same or worse problems and had not been fired. As a result, our client was reinstated to her position with full back pay.

In other cases, discrimination can be the result of a seemingly neutral policy. However, when that policy is further examined, it becomes clear that it has a disparate impact on members of certain ethnic groups. For example, an employer may require all applicants to pass a written exam. While this requirement may seem fair on its face, it may result in fewer minority applicants being eligible for employment. In that case, the employer's administration of such a test is an unlawful employment practice, unless it can demonstrate that the test is justified by business necessity.

Finally, in some cases, the discrimination doesn't come from a manager, but rather it emanates from co-workers. In these cases, co-workers can create a working atmosphere so hostile that it becomes impossible for the employee to fully concentrate on his or her job. This can occur when the employee is subjected to taunts, jeers and racial slurs. It can also happen when co-workers insist upon telling racist jokes or displaying offensive cartoons and drawings in the workplace. In these types of situations, the manager is obligated to put a stop to harassing behavior and if he or she does not, the victim of the harassment has a valid claim for racial discrimination.

Religion

These same general principles apply to cases of religious discrimination. For example, if a manager refuses to hire an applicant because "I just don't trust Jews" or refuses to promote an employee because "after 9/11, we have to be wary of all Muslims," he has committed an act of unlawful employment discrimination. Of course, as we discussed earlier, it's seldom that these types of sentiments will be voiced for others to hear. Yet, they can be proven with evidence that demonstrates that persons of a particular religion are treated differently than others.

More often, the discrimination in these types of cases is less overt. In fact, it's more like the disparate impact cases, in which a seemingly neutral policy results in problems in the workplace for certain workers. For example, a manager may request employees to work on Saturdays during particularly busy times of the year. However, a Jewish or Seventh Day Adventist employee who strictly observes the Sabbath will be unable to meet this request. In this type of situation, the manager may attempt to fire the employee or at least, come to view him or her as not being a "team player." This determination could lead the manager to pass over the employee for promotions, pay raises and other job-related benefits.

For this reason, under Title VII, this type of discrimination is not allowed. Federal employers are required by law to make *reasonable accommodations* for the religious observances and beliefs of their employees. Although the law in this area can be complicated at times, generally, the employer must accommodate an employee's religious observances unless there's a valid business justification for not doing so. Obviously, if the religious observance would result in the employee not being able to do his or her job or it would unduly disrupt the work of other employees, then the manager need not accommodate it. On the other hand, if the observance only requires violating some minor rule of the workplace, then the manager is required to accommodate it.

For instance, in the not-so-distant past, many employers had grooming policies that required employees to wear their hair a certain way or keep facial hair trimmed in a certain manner. Likewise, some of these policies prohibited employees from wearing earrings and having visible tattoos or markings. In many cases, these policies were in conflict with the religious observances of some employees. For instance, many religions require male observers to grow their hair much longer than would be allowed under these grooming policies. Under Title VII, unless the employer can demonstrate a compelling business justification for the grooming policy, an employee may not be discriminated against for failing to observe it.

We will discuss later the issue of religious compensatory time, which is a form of reasonable accommodation for religion in the federal sector. Generally, employees may earn and use religious compensatory time for religious observances, and absent proven undue hardship, agencies may not deny employees the right to earn or use religious comp time.

Gender

Discrimination on the basis of gender is treated like all other forms of discrimination under Title VII. Managers may not deny employment, promotions or other benefits to employees on the basis of their gender. As in other cases, discrimination can be proven by direct evidence of discrimination (e.g, "I can't hire you for this job. You're a woman!"), indirect evidence of discrimination (e.g., documentation illustrating that the complainant has been dealt with more harshly than persons of the opposite gender in similar situation) and disparate impact (e.g., only men have been promoted to managerial positions in a certain department over the last ten years).

In addition, employers may not discriminate against women on the basis of being pregnant. As a result, employers may not make hiring or promotion decisions based on the fact that the applicant is now pregnant or may become pregnant in the future. Also, employers must provide pregnant employees with the same benefits they would provide to any other person suffering from a temporary disability.

Finally, Title VII also covers claims of sexual harassment. As you probably know, there are two classic types of discrimination: (1) hostile work environment; and (2) *quid pro quo*. In the previous chapter, we discussed hostile work environment claims in some detail.

In a *quid pro quo* situation, the manager coerces or attempts to coerce the employee into a sexual relationship with the threat of workplace retribution or the promise of workplace benefits. For instance, a male manager might admonish a female employee that her work does not meet department expectations, but that she can make it up "in other ways". Or perhaps, a female manager might suggest to her male subordinate that if he wants to get ahead in the agency, he's going to have to learn to "play ball". Also, in recent years, an increasing number of cases have been brought by employees claiming same-sex *quid pro quo* offers. These types of offers are also unlawful employment practices and may be subject to Title VII action.

Finally, gender stereotyping is an illegal form of gender discrimination. If someone is discriminated against because he is "too feminine" or she is "too masculine," that could form the basis for Title VII liability.

Chapter 3

ADEA

The purpose of the Age Discrimination in Employment Act of 1967 (ADEA) is to promote employment of older persons and prevent arbitrary age discrimination in employment. As a result, a federal employer may not fire or refuse to hire a person on the basis of their age. Likewise, an employer may not condition the terms of employment based on age, including reducing an employee's salary once he or she reaches a certain age. Interestingly, the protections of the ADEA only apply to employees who are 40 years of age or older. In most jurisdictions, older employees are also protected from hostile work environments.

Sadly, age discrimination has become a major problem in both federal and private sector workplaces as some employers have attempted to "young-size" in an effort to reduce labor costs. As a general rule, older employees earn higher salaries and benefits due to their seniority and length of service with their employer. Some employers attempt to reduce their labor costs with respect to these employees by firing them, laying them off or coercing them into early retirement and then replacing them with younger (and presumably, less expensive) workers.

The ADEA is supposed to protect older employees from this type of discrimination. It also protects older employees from being subjected to discrimination from managers who mistakenly believe that older workers are less effective, more forgetful or more prone to become ill or injured on the job. Instead, under the ADEA, each employee must be judged on the basis of their skills and work record and not on the basis of their age. Recently, the US Supreme Court ruled that "disparate impact" claims may be brought under the ADEA as well as disparate treatment claims.

To pursue a claim of age discrimination under the ADEA, an employee or applicant must show that:

1. The employee is a member of the protected class (i.e., 40 years old or more);

2. The employee was qualified for the job for which he or she was

denied or terminated or laid off from or not promoted to;

3.   The employee was adversely affected by the employer's action; and

4.   The employer continued to seek younger applicants for the job with similar qualifications, or hired/promoted a younger individual.

"Younger" here means the other employee(s) or applicant(s) are under age 40 or substantially younger than the employee.

It should be noted that age discrimination can exist and is recognized as being illegal, even if *both* candidates are over 40, if one employee is "significantly older" than the other. For example, where the agency selects a 41-year-old for a promotion at the expense of a 57-year-old who was much more qualified, that employer may be liable for age discrimination.

Chapter 4

The Rehabilitation Act/ADA

The Rehabilitation Act of 1973 prohibits federal employers from discriminating against those with disabilities. Furthermore, federal employers must take affirmative steps to recruit disabled applicants and ensure that they are considered for vacancies and job training opportunities. Finally, federal employers must make reasonable accommodation for disabled employees. The Rehabilitation Act was the predecessor to the Americans with Disabilities Act (the "ADA"), which was signed into law in 1990. While the ADA ***does not apply directly*** to federal employees (the Rehab Act does), the standards and definitions in the ADA are incorporated into the Rehab Act, and therefore we use the two interchangeably in this book.

The purpose of the ADA/Rehab Act is to extend significant protections to people with disabilities, a record of a disability or who are perceived as being disabled. Under the ADA, a person is disabled if he or she has a physical or mental impairment that substantially limits one or more major life activities. While it is clear that a person who is blind, deaf or missing an arm is disabled for these purposes, other cases are not so clear. For example, people who suffer from less obvious or slightly less debilitating conditions like bi-polar disorder, carpal tunnel syndrome or back pain may not be considered "disabled" if their impairment doesn't *substantially* limit their ability to perform an activity that the average person in the general public can perform, or in the way that an average person performs it.

For purposes of the ADA, a history of drug or alcohol abuse is considered a disability in that a person may not be denied employment simply on the basis of being a recovering addict. However, to qualify for such protection, the employee or applicant must be truly in recovery and not still using drugs or alcohol. Furthermore, while an employer may not discriminate against an applicant because of his or her status as a recovering addict, the employer may take into account the person's past behavior while in its employ. For instance, if the applicant was previously employed by the employer and, due to their addiction, committed acts of fraud or negligence in the course of employment, the employer may take this into account when deciding whether to rehire or reinstate the employee.

It's important to understand that an employee may qualify as being disabled, as stated above, in one of three ways. He or she may be actually disabled, may have a record of impairment or may be simply perceived to be disabled.

A person is actually disabled if he or she is *substantially limited* from performing a major life activity. Please keep in mind that the courts have distinguished the term "substantially limited" from "moderately limited." For example, being *unable* to walk is a substantial limitation and therefore, someone with such a limitation would be protected under the ADA. On the other hand, not being able to walk long distances is only a moderate limitation and therefore, this "disability" may not, depending on the federal circuit, be entitled to protection under the ADA.

Perceived As Being Disabled

Likewise, a person who does not suffer from a condition that prohibits them performing or substantially limits them in performing a major life activity can still be deemed "disabled" for purposes of discrimination if they are *perceived* as having a disability. A common example of this type of designation is the employee who is perceived to be "crazy" by his co-workers and management.

In fact, we once had a case where we represented an employee who at one time suffered from carpal tunnel syndrome and was placed by the US Postal Service on light duty. A federal judge found that although the employee did not have an actual disability, she qualified for ADA protection by virtue of being perceived as having a disability.

Perceived as disabled cases often arise when an agency determines that an employee cannot safely perform his or her job, and the agency reassigns or terminates the employee. These cases are called "direct threat" cases and pose a significant burden upon the agency to prove that it performed an individualized assessment of the employee, the job, and possible accommodations that could alleviate the threat.

We had a case where the employee had sarcodoisis, and her agency fired her. A well-written 5-page letter describing her job, her impairment and potential accommodations the agency ignored was critical in having the employee immediately reinstated, with back pay and without having to go to a hearing.

In short, even if you don't have a disability, it is illegal for an agency to take any action against you if it *thinks* you have a disability.

Reassignment to a Vacant, Funded Position

Of course, even if an employee or applicant is "substantially limited," they are not entitled to protection if they cannot perform the *essential* functions of the job, unless there is another job that the employee can be reassigned to and which they can perform, with or without accommodation. What is an essential function, and whether a job can be restructured, are fact intensive inquiries and may require expert witness testimony.

We initially lost a case before an administrative judge because the client could not perform her job of interviewing the public. The administrative judge found that the agency couldn't do any more for our client than it had already done. We took the case up on appeal and had the ruling reversed. The EEOC Office of Federal Operations (OFO) found that the administrative judge erred in finding that the agency didn't have to reassign our client to a vacant, funded position which did not involve interviewing the public.

If the employee's disability prevents him or her from performing some *minor* function of a job, then the employer may not refuse to hire, promote or retain the employee on that basis. For example, if an applicant for an accounting position happens to be confined to a wheelchair, he or she can't be denied the position simply because, from time to time, the job requires the accountant to carry old files down to the storage room in the basement. Obviously, this occasional task is not an essential function of the job and therefore, if the applicant is otherwise qualified, he or she can't be denied on this basis.

On the other hand, if the accountant suffers from a condition causing permanent blurred vision, the employer may be able to deny him or her the position on this basis. This is particularly true if the position requires the applicant to be able to read ledgers and work papers.

Reasonable Accommodation

Of course, this assumes that the technology isn't available to enhance these materials so that the applicant can read them. Under the ADA, employers are required to make "reasonable accommodations" to assist the employee in carrying out his or her job duties. Examples of "reasonable accommodations" are as follows:

- A computer operator is involved in an automobile accident in which he injures his back. He is now unable to sit for long periods of time. In this case, a reasonable accommodation would be to provide the employee with a table tall enough to allow him to stand while working on the computer.

- A recovered alcoholic needs to take two hours for lunch each day to attend AA meetings. In this case, a reasonable accommodation would be to allow the employee to take the extra long lunches so long as he or she makes up the time at the beginning or end of the day.

To give another example, we recently had a client who was forced to file a complaint with the EEOC because her employer refused to make a reasonable accommodation in her case. She was a postal employee who was sensitive to temperature changes and despite repeated requests, her employer refused to control the extremely cold temperatures in her work area.

Please keep in mind that the employer need not make all accommodations for their disabled employees, just those that are reasonable. Therefore, the employer need not accommodate a disabled employee if doing so will create an undue hardship for the employer. Similarly, the agency does not have to provide a particular accommodation requested by an employee – only one that is "effective," even if the employee would prefer a different accommodation, even one that is more effective.

Finally, a failure to accommodate claim is only one kind of claim a disabled person may have. It is also unlawful for an employer to discriminate against a disabled employee in any tangible employment action or subject him or her to a hostile work environment. The ADA/Rehab Act also protects federal employees against impermissible medical inquiries, certain medical examinations, release of private medical information, handicapped parking and a variety of other actions.

Informal Interactive Process

One very important obligation often overlooked, or mismanaged, by agencies is the requirement (found in the EEOC's Guidance on Reasonable Accommodation under the Rehabilitation Act at www.eeoc.gov) that the agency engage a disabled employee in an "informal interactive process" to discuss how the agency can help accommodate the employee. Failure to sit down and discuss with an employee how the agency can help is a separate violation of the ADA. Of course, you have to cooperate with the agency as well in this process, or you could end up losing your case due to non-participation in the same informal interactive process.

Some agencies, like the USPS, have set up entire "Reasonable Accommodation Committees" with 10 or 20 members (including management, labor relations, and EEO and OGC attorneys) which look and feel more like an interrogation than an "informal interactive process." Don't be intimidated. Take a representative with you if you need one, bring your medical documentation with you if you have it, and be forceful about your disability and need for accommodation.

Chapter 5
The Equal Pay Act of 1963

Under the Equal Pay Act (EPA), employers may not discriminate in pay matters based upon gender. For instance, a federal agency may not pay men more than women for performing substantially equal jobs in the same organization. This law was passed to protect women from the outdated notion held by some managers that men should be paid more because they have families to support, or their work is more valuable, or some such nonsense. Of course, the law also protects men from being paid less than women doing substantially the same job in substantially the same manner.

However, even under this law, there are some situations in which unequal pay is permitted. For instance, unequal pay is allowed when it is due to differences in seniority, merit, or quantity and quality of production. As a result, a male employee in a job for thirty years might be lawfully paid more than a 2-year female employee in the same position. Of course, differences based on seniority and pay grade are often straightforward and easy to comprehend.

Therefore, the disputes in these cases often arise when the difference is based on perceived differences in the *quality* of production between male and female employees in the same position. Now, certainly, an employer is an entitled to more richly compensate an employee who provides a superior work product, but an employer may not use this measure as an excuse to make an end run around the EPA. In these types of cases, the dispute usually centers on the employer's ability to demonstrate that the pay differentiation is justified. In making these determinations, administrative judges will usually look to performance reviews and other "objective" job criteria to determine if such a performance difference truly exists.

Critical to proving an Equal Pay Act case is testimony from co-workers, and preferably testimony from someone in the position that you are comparing your work to. Also extremely helpful is expert witness testimony from a classification expert, who can analyze the type of work and method of work that you perform and compare it to the person of the opposite gender who is being paid more. Hopefully, they will testify that you are doing the same work and there's no reason to pay you less. If not, you can then reevaluate your case.

Chapter 6

Retaliation

While reading the previous chapters, you may have come to the inescapable conclusion that you've been the victim of unlawful discrimination in the workplace. If that's the case, then you're now faced with a decision – to accept it or to fight it? Needless to say, this is an enormous decision that could have career-altering consequences. Obviously, if you decide to fight for your rights, your decision will have repercussions. The same is true if you decide to do nothing, because your acceptance of the situation may embolden others to discriminate against you (and others) in the future.

Sadly, people sometimes opt to accept discrimination because they fear retaliation by their boss or other co-workers. And while this fear certainly isn't baseless, it shouldn't stop you from fighting for your rights. You have a *legal right* to work in an environment free from discrimination. Equally important; you have a legal right to be free from retaliation if you file a complaint.

Retaliation is illegal if it is a motivating factor in any action or threat, and the EEOC has held that a federal employee does not have to prove a 'tangible employment action' to win. Any action, or even a threat, will suffice. Of course, you still have to prove damages to get anything out of such a case, but retaliation cases can be easier to prove than disparate treatment or disparate impact cases. You are protected against retaliation if you file a complaint, if you protest what you reasonably believe is illegal discrimination, or if you are involved in the EEO process – even only as a witness.

Proving a Case of Retaliation

To prove a case of retaliation, you need to show that you "engaged" in protected activity, that the person taking the action knew about the protected activity, and that the action taken has a nexus to the protected activity. The last element can generally be shown by a proximity in time between the protected activity and the action taken against you. Like all other cases of discrimination, you have to seek EEO counseling within 45 days of when you know about the action or event that is retaliatory.

According to Section 8 of the EEOC Compliance Manual, it is the policy of the EEOC to ensure that "individuals who oppose unlawful employment discrimination, participate in employment discrimination proceedings, or otherwise assert their rights under the laws enforced by the Commission are protected against retaliation." As a result, an employer can't deny a promotion, refuse to hire, deny job benefits, demote, suspend, or discharge an employee for filing a complaint with the EEOC. Likewise, an employer may not threaten, reprimand, give negative evaluations or harass an employee in retaliation for filing a complaint. In fact, the anti-retaliation rules even apply to ex-employers. Therefore, an employer may not retaliate against a former employee by giving a negative job reference to a future employer.

Of course, this isn't to say that retaliation doesn't occur. Unfortunately, it happens quite frequently. We have had several cases where our clients were not only the victims of the original discriminatory actions, but also experienced subsequent retaliation after they filed a complaint. In fact, some employers have been found guilty of retaliation against individuals who hadn't even filed EEO complaints. These unfortunate employees had simply voiced their concerns about what they believed was discriminatory behavior and soon found themselves receiving poor performance reviews or being denied promotions or even being terminated for being "troublemakers."

Yet, that being the case, you still shouldn't be cowed by the prospect of retaliation. You have every right to stand up for yourself and fight back against discrimination. This right is recognized in the law and any retaliation by your boss or co-workers is a cause for additional damages and remedies.

Chapter 7

An Overview of the EEO Complaint Process

Interestingly, deciding to fight for your rights is just one part of the decision making process. You must also choose a forum in which to wage your battle. While this book is mainly concerned with helping you to fight (and win) before an EEOC Administrative Judge, you may be forced to bring your case to a different body, or you may have choices available to you, depending on the type of claim and other factors.

Claims Required to Go to the MSPB

For example, you may have to bring your case before the Merit Systems Protection Board (MSPB). The MSPB is an independent quasi-judicial agency established to ensure adequate protection for many federal civilian employees against abuses by agency management. Among its many charges is to adjudicate employee appeals of personnel actions, such as removals, suspensions, WIGI denials, RIFs, furloughs, and demotions.

Therefore, if you've been unjustly terminated, demoted, suspended for 15 days or more, RIFed, or denied disability retirement, you may have to bring your claim to the MSPB. This does not apply to probationary employees or non-managerial USPS employees, who can bring termination, demotion and long term suspension cases directly to the EEOC. A claim of discrimination can be brought to the MSPB (it is then called a "mixed case"), which will look at the adverse action and the discrimination claim together. For MSPB cases, look for our forthcoming book, "Fight For Your Rights II: A Federal Employee's Do-It-Yourself Guide to MSPB Hearings and Appeals."

Suffice it to say that you can either claim discrimination in an appeal to the MSPB (which must be filed within 30 days, not 45), or you can file for EEO Counseling and file an EEO Complaint, and your agency should flag the case as a "mixed case" and issue an ROI and a Final Agency Decision, which can then be appealed to the MSPB.

Bargaining Unit Employees & EEO Grievances

Likewise, if you are a Bargaining Unit employee (you can tell by looking at the "Bargaining Unit code" on any SF-50), that means you are represented by a federal employee union. In that case, 99% of the time your union will have bargained a grievance procedure that allows you to bring a claim of discrimination through the grievance process. Be aware that you don't have the same "right" to a hearing – only the union can take a case to an arbitrator, who is often far less experienced than an EEO Administrative Judge. There may be other reasons to take a case to arbitration rather than to an EEO AJ, like a contractual violation of the CBA that is easier to prove. Be very careful to not file a Grievance and an EEO Complaint on the same issue, since (except for USPS employees) you can only pursue one or the other. The same goes for filing a Grievance vs. an MSPB appeal – the earlier one filed will block you from the other avenue.

Discrimination claims can be included in cases before the EEOC, MSPB and arbitrators (to the extent that they are available to you). However, you may not bring your claim in more than one forum.

In other words, you can't have your cake and eat it too; particularly, not with respect to EEO claims. Once you take your claim before the MSPB or once a Grievance is filed, you will be barred from going through the EEO process (at least, until the appeals process). For that reason, it's extremely important to decide the proper forum for your dispute.

To help you in making this decision, we will give you a brief overview of the entire EEO process in this chapter. The point here is to give you an idea of the possible road ahead so you can determine for yourself if this is the right route for you. Of course, by this point, you may be already well into the process. However, even if this is the case, this overview will help you to plan for your hearing or take the next steps after the hearing.

After this overview, we will go into a more detailed explanation of the process, with tips, hints and forms along the way.

Contacting an EEO Counselor

The first step in the process is to set up a meeting with an EEO Counselor. The name and contact information for this individual should be posted in the workplace. You must contact the Counselor within 45 days of the discriminatory action in order to avail yourself of the process.

In a sense, the EEO Counselor is the gatekeeper to the entire EEO process. You must first meet with this person before you can file a formal complaint with the agency or even a lawsuit alleging violations of Title VII.

You can contact the EEO office by phone, in person or by email. You should always make a note of when you first made contact, since that will be the "anchor date" for your complaint, and may prove very critical at later stages in your case. If you are going in person, you can bring a witness. Email is a good way of creating a paper trail. Some agencies have full-time EEO Counselors. Others use EEO Counselors who perform agency work most of the time and EEO counseling duties part-time, which are "collateral duties" for them. Some agencies have EEO Counselors on-site in every office, and others have centralized all EEO functions into their headquarters or some other office. The contact information is supposed to be posted clearly in the workplace, usually in the lunchroom or on a bulletin board.

Many EEO Counselors are very busy, and you might not get to meet with one right away. Some of them will ask you right away for an extension of time (they only have 30 days to finish their initial report, and cannot extend the time without your permission). We sometimes advise clients not to allow an extension, depending on the case.

After your initial meeting with the counselor, he or she will conduct a limited inquiry by making contact with the responsible agency person(s) involved. During this time period, the counselor is supposed to attempt to find some way for you and the agency to resolve the dispute without moving on to the next stage of the process – the formal complaint. In doing so, the counselor sometimes will inform you of alternative dispute resolution methods, such as mediation, mini-trials and the like. More often, the counselor takes a statement from you describing the problem, the basis for your complaint (gender, race, etc.) and what you are seeking as a resolution. The counselor then usually takes your version of events and your requested relief to the Responsible Management Official (RMO) and presents it to them to get their reaction. The counselor often takes their statement of what occurred and their rejection of your relief, and any offer they may have to resolve the case, and types it all up.

You should make sure to give the counselor a detailed description of what occurred, since the accepted issue for investigation is often based not only upon the complaint, but also upon the counselor's report.

If no resolution has been reached, then the counselor will meet with you for a final interview. At the final interview, the counselor will review what occurred during the counseling process and inform you of your right to file a formal complaint with the EEOC. Most EEO Counselors will issue a "Final Counseling Report" at this meeting, but the Department of Veterans Affairs is one agency we have found that won't release this document to you until after you have filed a Formal Complaint.

The Formal Complaint

You have 15 days from the date of the final interview to file your Formal Complaint with a designated person at the federal agency for which you are employed. Shortly after the filing of the complaint, the agency will send you an acceptance letter listing the claims you've asserted and the claims it will be investigating. Unfortunately, these lists aren't always identical, as the agency may choose to dismiss some (or all) of your claims, for reasons we will discuss in detail in a later chapter.

Nevertheless, the agency has only 180 days from the filing of your complaint to complete its investigation of the remaining claims. During this time period, an EEO Investigator (either in-house or a contractor) is supposed to build a factual record by interviewing the persons involved and other witnesses. The investigator may also request documents and records from the parties.

If the agency fails to complete its investigation within the required time period, you are then free to force the matter in one of two ways: (1) You can request a hearing before an administrative judge; or (2) You can file a civil suit in federal court. Otherwise, upon completion of the investigation, the agency will provide you with a copy of the factual record (often called a "Report of Investigation" or ROI, or at DoD facilities, an "Investigative File."). At this point, you will have one of two choices: (1) Request a hearing before an administrative judge; or (2) Request a Final Agency Decision (FAD) by the agency. In either event, you will have moved to the next stage of the process – the decision stage. Of course, at any time prior to this point, you and the agency are free to resolve your dispute.

If you fail to request a hearing, the agency will issue a FAD, after which you can then go to court or appeal the FAD to the EEOC's appellate division, the Office of Federal Operations. Instructions will be included in the FAD for all of these options.

The Hearing

The hearing is a trial presided over by an administrative judge. Prior to the hearing, the administrative judge will usually attempt to review the factual record and sort out those matters which are still subject to dispute between the parties. The administrative judge may also allow time for additional discovery, whereby each party is allowed to conduct a further examination of the matter by requesting information from the other party. During this pre-hearing process, the administrative judge may dismiss part (or all) of the complaint or rule in your favor if there are no facts in dispute. If there are facts in dispute, such as conflicting witness testimony, then the administrative judge is supposed to convene a hearing. At the conclusion of the hearing, the administrative judge will issue a decision.

EEOC Final Action

Ironically, this may not be the end of the matter. Even if the administrative judge rules in your favor, the agency has 40 days to review the decision and take action by issuing a formal order. It isn't uncommon in this situation for the agency to modify the administrative judge's decision, such as by reducing the recovery of back wages or front pay, or completely vacating the decision and issuing a final order denying discrimination has occurred. If this occurs, then the agency is supposed to simultaneously file an appeal with the EEOC's OFO. You will then have the opportunity to respond to the agency's appeal. If the administrative judge rules in favor of the agency, then you still have two avenues for appeal: (1) an EEOC appeal; or (2) a civil lawsuit in federal court.

Appeal

You have 30 days from the date of receiving a notice of final action (or FAD) to file an appeal with the EEOC. Please note that this appeal right (and the accompanying 30-day time frame) applies to all types of final actions, including the dismissal of claims during the investigative or hearing process. In other words, any adverse ruling that applied along the way can be appealed at this stage, although you may not have had the opportunity to appeal them earlier (such as an early dismissal of a claim).

In support of your appeal, you may file a brief or statement within 30 days of filing your appeal. The agency may file a brief or statement in opposition to your appeal within 30 days of receiving your brief or statement.

Review of AJ Decisions – Limited in Scope

The appeal of an administrative judge's decision is a very limited inquiry. In most cases, the EEOC won't allow you to introduce new facts or call for the testimony of witnesses. In reaching its decision, the EEOC will give deference to the administrative judge's interpretation of the facts. In fact, if any reasonable person could have concluded as the administrative judge did, then that conclusion will stand. However, the EEOC will overturn the administrative judge's decision if it is based on a faulty interpretation of the law.

On the other hand, appeals from a FAD issued due to the request of an employee, due to failure to request a hearing, or from agency final actions that are inconsistent with the administrative judge's decision, are treated differently. In those cases, the EEOC reviews the factual record "de novo," or from scratch. It then takes the facts as it sees them and applies the proper law.

Civil Lawsuits

Finally, you are given the option of taking your claim outside the EEO process and litigating your case in federal court. For instance, if the agency fails to investigate your complaint within the 180-day time period, you can file a civil suit. Furthermore, rather than file an appeal with the EEOC, you can file suit within 90 days of the agency's final action. And even if you file an appeal with the EEOC, you can still take your case to federal court if you lose the appeal or simply if the EEOC fails to rule within 180 days of your filing the appeal.

A complete overview of the process is illustrated at the end of this chapter (from the Department of Health and Human Services). As you can see, the EEOC process can be quite complex and can take anywhere from a few months to a few years to work your way through it. That being the case, before embarking on the journey, you will want to make an honest assessment of your claim of discrimination.

First of all, have you really been the victim of unlawful discrimination or is there some more plausible reason why you were fired, not hired, transferred or didn't get the promotion you were seeking? Second, can you prove your case? Third, what type of damages can you reasonably recover?

Answering these questions will require a level-headed and dispassionate look at the situation. Perhaps, at this point, you may wish to consult with an attorney who concentrates in this area of the law to provide you with some feedback. He or she can provide you with a knowledgeable assessment of the merits of your case and even provide tips on the best way to go about proving it.

Once you have a realistic view of your case, then the only other factor left in making your decision is *you*. Are you willing to make the investment in time and effort necessary to see your case through to the end? This may largely depend upon your future career plans with your employer.

For example, if you're planning on leaving your job next month to spend more time with your kids, then it probably doesn't make sense to fight your unlawful denial of just a single training opportunity. If you've been cheated out of something much more valuable, or if you have been damaged much more severely, you may choose to fight the case, even if you are no longer employed. As another example, if you're planning to make a career in civil service, the denial of a promotion that you've *earned* makes a big difference. It will affect your ability to seek other promotions, which will have a long-term effect on your pay grade and ultimately, your pension benefits. The stakes in this case are certainly high enough to be worth the effort. Or, denial of an accommodation often forces employees to either work in great pain or with great difficulty, or be forced to apply for OWCP or disability retirement.

OVERVIEW OF EEO COMPLAINT PROCESS

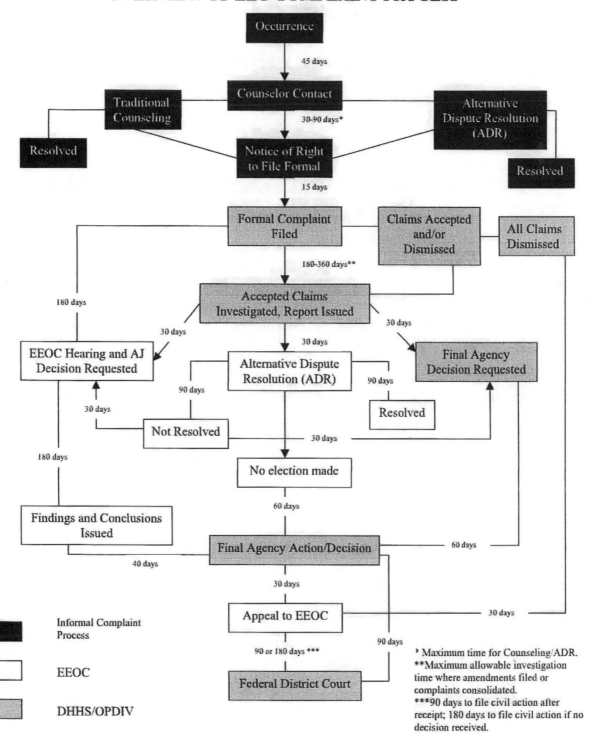

Chapter 8

Getting Started in the EEO Process

The Initial Contact

Assuming that you've decided to move forward with your discrimination claim, the first step is to contact an EEO Counselor. The name and contact information for this individual should be clearly posted in your workplace, often on a bulletin board and/or the agency's website. If that's not the case, then you can find this information by visiting your agency's EEO office or the office that handles personnel issues.

Remember, you *only* have 45 days from the date of the discriminatory action to contact the counselor. In far too many cases, victims of discrimination let this time period lapse thinking that perhaps the discriminatory action is just an isolated incident. Finally, only when a series of these incidents has occurred, do they decide to contact an EEO Counselor.

However, in many cases, the agency will challenge the victim's right to embark on the EEO process because the first incident occurred more than 45 days before filing the complaint. At the very least, the agency may argue that the ensuing investigation should only include new events of discrimination that occurred within the 45-day window.

In this situation, as the victim of discrimination, you may be able to salvage some of your prior claims. However, to do so, you will have to demonstrate that the events were all related and continuing in nature. For instance, if you've been the victim of ongoing sexual harassment at the hands of the same person (or group of people), then you should be able to preserve your claims for all incidents of harassment, even those that occurred more than 45 days before contacting the EEO Counselor.

Of course, from a legal standpoint, it's best not to wait. Nonetheless, since we don't live in a legal vacuum, you may not feel the need to contact an EEO Counselor after the first incident of discrimination. However, keep in mind that if the 45-day period lapses, you may forfeit your right to *ever* bring a claim regarding this action.

Of course, your delay may be justified if you don't find out about the discriminatory action until much later, or if you didn't know about the 45-day requirement at all. For example, if you applied for a promotion and didn't find out about not being selected for two months, your contact will be timely as long as it is made within 45 days of when you first knew (or had reason to know) that you were not selected.

However, the situation might turn out differently if you *knew* about the non-selection but contacted your counselor four months later only when you found out that the recommending official told someone, "Yeah, it's certainly a good thing we hired a black person for that promotion. We certainly don't want Jesse Jackson coming after us." Even though you had absolutely no suspicion that discrimination was involved, your contact may be deemed untimely because it was filed more than 45 days after you knew you didn't get selected for the promotion.

The cases on this point are extremely fact-specific and therefore, the analysis of your particular situation could go either way. However, it's better to not take any chances. Contact an EEO Counselor immediately upon learning of an event which *could* be discriminatory. Don't sit on your rights. You can even pursue EEO counseling anonymously, if you just want to discover enough facts to decide whether to move forward or not.

Interestingly, in some cases, you may not discover the discriminatory action took place until some time later. For instance, it may take several weeks for you to be notified about not getting a promotion you deserved. Or in some cases, you may be the unknowing victim of discrimination and not realize that you lost a promotion or training opportunity due to your race, gender or religion until you overhear a conversation at the water cooler six months later. Fortunately, federal law provides an extension to the 45-day time period if you "did not know or reasonably should not have known that the discriminatory matter or personal action occurred."

Also, the 45-day window will be expanded if you miss it for reasons beyond your control. For example, if the time period elapses while you are lying in a hospital bed in critical condition, your tardiness in contacting the counselor probably will be excused.

All of that being said, your initial contact with the EEO Counselor can be made in person, by phone, by email or through another method. Since the date of your first contact with a counselor is such a critical date, you will want to send him or her an email (with a return receipt) or a fax confirming your contact. Also, make sure that you make a written record of your conversation in your diary or appointment book.

The Initial Interview

Once you contact the EEO Counselor, he or she will arrange a time for your initial interview. At the interview, the counselor will explain your rights and responsibilities under the EEO process. The counselor is also bound by law to provide you with a written Notice of Rights and Responsibilities. He or she may ask you to acknowledge that you received the form by signing and dating it at the bottom. On the next few pages, we provided a form of this notice so that you won't be confused or intimidated if you're asked to sign an unfamiliar document. Some agencies use a rather lengthy checklist and ask you to initial next to dozens of statements. A word to the wise: read each statement **carefully** before signing or initialing, and **always** get a copy of anything you sign or initial.

The counselor will also ask for your statement of what happened. Specifically, he or she will want to know what happened (i.e., the tangible employment action you claim happened), upon what <u>basis</u> you believe you've been discriminated against (e.g., race, gender, etc.) and what <u>evidence</u> you have to support your claim. It's important to remember that your counselor can only handle cases of unlawful discrimination arising under Title VII, the ADEA, the Rehab Act (which applies the same standards as the ADA) and the EPA. Therefore, you should make every effort to clearly demonstrate why your claim falls under one of these laws and provide the counselor with as much evidence as possible to support your claim of discrimination.

EEO Counselors typically type up your statement, present it to you for your review and signature, and then tell you that they are going to management to try and resolve the issues you have raised.

Alternative Dispute Resolution

At the initial interview, the counselor will also explain the counseling process and likely, offer you the opportunity to either pursue the standard EEO counseling process or to attempt to resolve your dispute outside of this process.

It's entirely possible that you will be offered an alternative dispute resolution (ADR) method as a quick way to solve your problem. After all, the formal complaint process will probably take six months at a minimum – even before you get to a hearing. A good number of informal complaints are resolved through ADR (some agencies claim as high as 60%), and you can find many good books about mediation in your agency or public library.

WRITTEN NOTICE OF RIGHTS AND RESPONSIBILITIES

1. Precomplaint counseling initiated on _____, will end in 30-days on _____, when I shall issue a Notice of Final Interview (NOFI). (An extension of precomplaint counseling, not to exceed 60-days, may be granted only upon written permission from the Equal Employment Opportunity Officer.) You have the right to file a formal complaint of discrimination within 15-days after I issue the NOFI.

2. The primary purpose of the precomplaint counseling which began on is to seek a solution to the matters which you brought to my attention. As the assigned EEO Counselor, <u>I am not your advocate in this endeavor</u>, nor am I an advocate for the Department. I will make necessary inquiries and counsel you concerning the issues in the matters you may raise.

3. You have the right to be represented by a person of your choice at any time during administrative complaint procedures, including this precomplaint counseling. If you obtain representation, you must notify the appropriate EEO Office, in writing, of the name and address of your representative, immediately upon obtaining the representative. Failure to so notify this office may result in loss of attorney's fees to which you may otherwise have been entitled.

4. You have the right to remain anonymous during this period of precomplaint counseling unless you give me specific written permission to reveal your identity. The matters you brought to my attention may be more readily resolved if you permit the use of your name during this precomplaint counseling.

5. If you believe that you have been subjected to unlawful discrimination because of your race, color, national origin, religion, handicapping condition, sex, sexual orientation[1] or reprisal for participation in activity protected by the Equal Employment Opportunity Act or the Rehabilitation Act; you must first follow administrative complaint processing procedures before you appeal to the Equal Employment Opportunity Commission (EEOC), Merit Systems Protection Board (MSPB*), or file a civil action in a U.S. District Court. [Note: "Filing a civil action under § 1614.408 or § 1614.409 shall terminate Commission processing of the appeal. If private suit is filed subsequent to the filing of an appeal, the parties are requested to notify the Commission in writing." 29 CFR 1614.410]

6. You are entitled to a reasonable amount of official time to present your complaint pursuant to 29 C.F.R. § 1614.605(b). In order to receive official time it must be requested and in order to be eligible to receive official time, you must be in an active duty status with the Agency.

7. Allegations of discrimination grounded in acts or events occurring more than 45-days prior to _____ may be dismissed as untimely filed by the Director, Office for Equal Opportunity pursuant to 29 CFR 1614.107 (b).

8. Allegations of discrimination grounded in acts, events or matters which you have initiated through an internal grievance procedure, negotiated grievance procedure, a previously filed EEO Complaint, filed in U.S. District Court, appealed to the MSPB*, etc., will be dismissed by the Director, Office for Equal Opportunity pursuant to 29 CFR 1614.107 (d).

9. If the matters which you bring to my attention are not resolved to your satisfaction, you may file a formal complaint of discrimination no later than 15-days after I issue the NOFI.

10. I will prepare a Counselor's Report at the conclusion of pre- complaint counseling and submit it to the Chief Counselor or the Equal Employment Opportunity Officer.

11. You may file a formal complaint only on those matters which you specifically bring to my attention during these 30-days of precomplaint counseling. Other matters may be dismissed by the Director, Office for Equal Opportunity pursuant to 29 CFR 1614.107 (b).

12. If you file a formal complaint of discrimination and the Department of the Interior fails to issue a Final Decision within 180-days of filing your formal complaint, you may file a civil action in U.S. District Court.

13. If you believe that you have been subjected to unlawful age discrimination (over 40), you may, 30-days after filing a "notice of intent to sue" with the EEOC, file a civil action in U.S. District Court without going through administrative complaint procedures. If you choose to pursue allegations of age discrimination administratively, you must first exhaust administrative procedures, including appeals to the EEOC or MSPB, before filing a civil action in U.S. District Court.

14. Your formal complaint will be acknowledged.

15. If your formal complaint, or any portion thereof, is dismissed the Director, Office for Equal Opportunity will inform you in writing of your appeal rights.

16. If your formal complaint is accepted for processing, the acceptance letter will specifically state your allegation[s] of discrimination, and provide specific information regarding the processing of your complaint and appeal rights. You will receive a copy of the Counselor's Report, and your complaint will be investigated. The Department of the Interior must issue the report of investigation no later than 180-days after you file your complaint. [29 CFR 1614.108(f)]

17. Upon completion of the investigation, the Investigator will prepare a Report of Investigation, a copy of which will be provided to you by the Equal Employment Opportunity Officer.

18. Upon receipt of the Report of Investigation, you may request a hearing before an EEOC Administrative Judge or a final decision without a hearing. Your written request must be made to Director, Office for Equal Opportunity within 30-days of your receipt of the report of investigation. If you make no request, you will receive a final decision without a hearing within 90-days of your receipt of the report of investigation

19. If you request a decision without a hearing, you should receive a final decision within 60-days of your request.

20. If you request a hearing, a hearing will be conducted by an Administrative Judge from the Equal Employment Opportunity Commission in accordance with 29 CFR 1614.109.

21. The Administrative Judge will send copies of findings, conclusions, and orders along with the entire record, by certified mail, return receipt requested, to you and to this agency within 180-days of the Commission's receipt of your request for a hearing.

22. After the hearing, the Administrative Judge will issue a "recommended decision" which the Director, Office for Equal Opportunity may adopt, modify or reject in the Final Decision. The Administrative Judge's findings of fact, conclusions of law and orders for relief become the final decision 60-days after receipt unless rejected or modified in writing by this agency in a final decision. The Final Decision closes administrative processing of your complaint within the Department.

23. If you are not satisfied with the Final Decision, you may appeal the matter to the EEOC, or you may file a civil action in U.S. District Court. The final agency decision will give you detailed information necessary to exercise appeal rights.

24. If you appeal to EEOC and are dissatisfied with the appellate decision, you may request that the Commission reconsider its decision, or you may file a civil action in U.S. District Court.

* If your formal complaint raises allegations within the appellate jurisdiction of the Merit Systems Protection Board (such as termination of employment, denial of within grade increase, demotion, RIF, suspension for more than 14-days, furlough for less than 30-days, "constructive discharge," etc.), it is known as a mixed case complaint. The following procedures apply to mixed case complaints: (See 5 CFR 1201 for details.)

1.   You may file a mixed case appeal of the matter (including allegations of unlawful discrimination) directly to the MSPB without filing a formal complaint of discrimination and going through the administrative complaint process. Mixed case appeals must be filed no later than 20-days after the effective date of the matter giving rise to the appeal. The MSPB decision will be binding on all parties.

2   If you file a mixed case complaint, processing will follow steps 12-17 above, and your appeal rights will be to the MSPB, not to the EEOC.

3.   The Final Decision to your mixed case complaint will be issued without a hearing. You may appeal the Final Decision of a mixed case complaint to the MSPB, or file a civil action in U.S. District Court. The MSPB will conduct a hearing if your appeal is timely filed and alleges unlawful discrimination.

4.   If you are not satisfied with the MSPB decision to your mixed case complaint, you may file a petition with EEOC, or file a civil action in U.S. District Court.

I have been informed of the employee's/applicant's rights by the EEO Counselor on
_____.

_____ _____
Signature [Aggrieved] Date

If you do choose to use the ADR process, you may want to take a representative with you, because often a mediator (paid for by the agency) can exert significant pressure to force a settlement. Therefore, you could use someone on your side to give advice and help you think clearly.

Also, you should note that the ADR process extends the initial counseling timeframe from 30 days to 90 days. If a settlement hasn't been reached in this extended time period, then you are free to move to the next step in the process – filing a formal complaint with the agency.

The Informal Inquiry

After the initial interview is complete, your counselor will begin the informal inquiry. In doing so, he or she will interview the alleged discriminating party and possibly even witnesses to the discrimination, if any. If at all possible, the counselor is supposed to make the inquiry on a confidential basis without revealing your identity. Yet, in many cases, it will be necessary to reveal your identity. And even if you're not named specifically, it will often be obvious who the complaining party is; particularly if you've previously complained about the discriminatory practice.

Early Resolution of Your Case

You should be aware that the counselor has a mandate from the EEOC to resolve these types of disputes as quickly as possibly. According to an EEOC Management Directive, "[i]n almost all instances, informal resolution, freely arrived at by all parties involved in the dispute, is the best outcome of a counseling action." Perhaps it's not surprising then, that in 2003, **less than 40%** of the more than 45,000 complaints filed ever reached the formal complaint stage.

Now, in pushing for resolution, the counselor is supposed to remain neutral and, according to the Management Directive, "not inject his/her views on settlement negotiations." However, this doesn't always happen. In fact, our clients often tell us that they were urged by counselors to drop their complaint because, in the counselor's words, "they didn't have a case."

If you should encounter such sentiments from your counselor, try to take them with a grain of salt. Understand that the counselor is attempting to fulfill his or her mandate of resolving these matters prior to the formal complaint stage and an easy way to do that is to convince you to drop your case. Therefore, don't allow yourself to be bullied into sacrificing your rights on the altar of informal resolution. If you've been the victim of discrimination and you believe you can back up your claim with facts, then stick to your guns. If necessary, you may want to have a lawyer concentrating in this field to independently review the merits of your case and provide you with a second opinion.

That being said, you should give the resolution process a chance. At the initial interview, your counselor may ask you, "What would it take for you to be satisfied?" If your dispute can easily be resolved by, say, your manager allowing you to participate in a particular training project, then say so. If the law and facts are on your side, your boss may quickly realize that it is in his or her best interests to deal fairly with you, especially if the costs of doing so are not very high. Unfortunately, rationality won't always prevail in these situations, but it's worth a try anyway.

To encourage both you and your employer to fully participate in the pre-complaint resolution process, the counselor isn't supposed to report the specifics of settlement discussions you may have had with your employer. Counselors are discouraged from doing so to encourage you and your employer to make offers and concessions without fear that they could be used against you at a later time. Nevertheless, nearly all counselors routinely include a full description of attempts at resolution. The first thing an AJ usually sees is that the complainant requested "$300,000.00," since that is the maximum in non-pecuniary damages that can be recovered. It looks much better to request "reasonable compensatory damages" than to look like you are either over-reaching or don't realize the true value of your damages.

Therefore, be sure to keep in mind that you shouldn't say anything in the pre-complaint resolution discussions that you wouldn't want to be read by the agency or an administrative judge at a later date in the proceedings. Needless to say, you should be extremely careful in remaining consistent in your version of the facts. Of course, the easiest way to do so is to tell the truth. Not only is it the right thing to do. but it's the easiest because there is only one version of the facts you have to remember.

This is good advice even if you discover that agency witnesses are fudging the truth (or worse). Many times, you will be able to trip them up with their inconsistent statements to the counselor and the EEO Investigator.

If you and your employer come to a resolution during the 30-day inquiry period, your counselor will draft a resolution letter setting forth the terms of the arrangement and detailing your options if the agency somehow fails to live up to its obligations under the agreement. This letter is usually signed by the counselor, the agency and you. We've provided a sample of this letter on the next page.

Of course, it goes without saying that you should make sure that the letter accurately reflects the terms of your agreement. You shouldn't just assume that the counselor "got it right." Also, make sure that you keep a copy of this letter for your files. This may be important later if the agency doesn't fully live up to its obligations under the settlement. In that case, you will have to notify the Director of Equal Employment Opportunity of the violation and allow the agency an opportunity to fix it. If they don't, you can go to the EEOC's OFO and request that your agreement be enforced or that the agency resume further processing of your EEO claim. In either case, having a copy of the informal resolution letter will be necessary to make your case that the agency isn't living up to its end of the bargain.

Keeping the Ball Rolling

On the other hand, if you're unable to come to a resolution with your employer, then the counselor must hold a final interview with you by the end of the 30-day investigation period. Remember, the counselor has *only 30 days* from the date you initiated contact to complete the informal inquiry. While your counselor is supposed to make every effort to resolve your dispute within this time frame, it's unlikely that he or she will do so. The sad truth is that many counselors are either overloaded or handle EEO matters as a "collateral duty." As a result, they rarely, if ever, meet the 30-day requirement.

As a result, your counselor will, in some cases, ask you for one or more 30-day extensions. You are free to grant or reject this request for an extension. If you feel that a few extra days may help you to resolve the matter, then you may want to grant the extension. On the other hand, if you feel that another 30 days won't help move the matter forward, then feel free to deny the extension request and push for your final interview and right to request a hearing.

It's important for you to be firm in this latter situation because if you don't, the initial counseling period could drag on for months; if not *years*. As amazing as it may sound, we had a client who filed for informal counseling eight times over three years, and the agency failed to give counseling for *any* of these informal complaints. Simply put, you can't put too much trust in the system. You must be proactive. Keep on the counselor and if he or she is late, even by a day, don't hesitate to take your case to the next level.

SAMPLE RESOLUTION LETTER

Jane Doe
123 Main Street
Anytown, USA 12345

        Re: Resolution of EEO Dispute

Dear Jane Doe:

This refers to the dispute which you first discussed with me on _____
when you alleged discrimination because of _____
when on _____ the following occurred:

_____
_____
_____

The purpose of this letter is to set out the terms of the informal resolution, which is as follows:

_____
_____
_____
_____

If you believe the Agency has not complied with the terms of the informal resolution, you may, under 29 C.F.R. § 1614.504, notify the Director of Equal Employment Opportunity in writing within 30 days of the date of the alleged violation, requesting that the terms of the informal agreement be specifically implemented. Alternatively, you may request that the claim be reinstated for further processing from the point processing ceased.

The Agency has signed the terms of the resolution as indicated by the signature of the Agency official. Your signature and date below will verify your receipt of this letter and will signify your agreement with the terms of the informal resolution of this dispute as set forth above. Enclosed is a duplicate copy of this letter. Please date and sign the original and the copy in the spaces provided and return the copy to me for inclusion in the counseling file. I will send a signed copy to the Agency. You may keep the original.

Sincerely,

_____   _____   _____
EEO Counselor   Agency Official   Aggrieved Person
Date: Date: Date:

The Final Interview

At the final interview, the Counselor is required to advise you in writing of your right to file a formal complaint. A sample of this notice is printed on the next two pages.

Also, in most agencies, you will receive the entire Counseling Report from the counselor prior to filing a formal complaint. In some agencies (like the VA), the agency will not give you a copy of the Counseling Report until *after* you file your formal complaint. Of course, this latter method makes little or no sense and likely increases the percentage of cases that go to the formal stage. Nevertheless, the Counseling Report usually will be delivered to you along with the Notice of Final Interview and Notice of Rights.

Sometimes, the final interview is done in person. Other times, the notice of final interview is mailed to you by the agency.

NOTICE OF RIGHT TO FILE A DISCRIMINATION COMPLAINT

SUBJECT: Notice of Right to File a Discrimination Complaint

FROM: [EEO Counselor]

TO: Jane Doe

This is to inform you that because the dispute you brought to my attention has not been resolved to your satisfaction, you are now entitled to file an individual or class-based discrimination Complaint based on race, color, religion, sex, national origin, physical or mental disability, age, and/or reprisal. If you file a Complaint, it must be in writing, signed, and filed within fifteen (15) calendar days after the receipt of the notice, with any of the following officials authorized to receive discrimination Complaints.

- Field Installation Head

  _____
  _____
  _____
  _____

- Agency Director of Equal Employment Opportunity

  _____
  _____
  _____
  _____

- Agency Head

  _____
  _____
  _____
  _____

- Other Official(s) as designated by the Agency, for example, an Agency Equal Employment Opportunity Officer, the Hispanic Program Coordinator, the Disability Program Coordinator, or the Federal Women's Program Coordinator

  _____
  _____
  _____
  _____

A Complaint shall be deemed timely if it is received or postmarked before the expiration of the 15-day filing period, or in the absence of a legible postmark, if it is received by mail within five days of the expiration of the filing period.

If you file your Complaint with one of the officials listed above (other than the EEO officer), it will be sent to the activity EEO officer for processing. Therefore, if you choose to file your Complaint with any of the other officials listed above, be sure to provide a copy of your Complaint to the EEO officer to ensure prompt processing of your Complaint.

The Complaint must be specific and contain only those issues either specifically discussed with me or issues that are like or related to the issues that you discussed with me. It must also state whether you have filed a grievance under a negotiated grievance procedure or an appeal to the Merit Systems Protection Board on the same claims.

If you retain an attorney or any other person to represent you, you or your representative must immediately notify the EEO officer, in writing. You and/or your representative will receive a written acknowledgment of your discrimination Complaint from the appropriate Agency official.

If you file a Complaint, you should name _____.

_____
EEO Counselor

Chapter 9
The Formal Complaint

Timing of the Complaint

Assuming that the matter wasn't resolved during the counseling process, you have 15 days from the date of your final interview to file your formal complaint. For purposes of meeting this deadline, the formal complaint is considered received when it is placed in the mail or hand-delivered. For example, if you have your final interview on July 15th, you have until July 30th to put your complaint in the mail (or have it hand-delivered). However, if July 30th falls a holiday or weekend day (Saturday or Sunday), you have until the next business day to make your filing.

It's **_very important_** that you meet this deadline because it is strictly enforced. There are no extensions or late fees. If you fail to file your formal complaint in time, you will not only forfeit your right to utilize the EEO process, but you will also forfeit your right to file a lawsuit in federal court. In short, if you snooze, you lose.

There are only three ways of bringing your case if you miss the deadline. The first way is to demonstrate that you never received notice of your right to file a complaint from the EEO Counselor. However, usually the notice is given at the final interview or mailed to you by certified mail. Another way to be able to bring your case after missing the deadline is to demonstrate that you were totally incapacitated (e.g., in a coma, on a respirator, etc.) during the 15-day period. Finally, if you have filed on a continuing violation or continuous hostile work environment claim, you can contact an EEO Counselor and start the process over from the beginning (assuming a new incident happened in the 45 days prior to the new contact with an EEO Counselor).

Form of Your Complaint

The federal government has tens of thousands of forms to cover almost any occasion, so it should be no surprise to you that there are dozens of different forms used for filing a formal EEO complaint. Just about every agency has its own form. On the next page, you will find one of these forms.

FORMAL COMPLAINT OF DISCRIMINATION IN THE FEDERAL GOVERNMENT

AUTHORITY:	42 U.S.C. 2000e-16(b) and (c); 29 U.S.C. Chapter 14; E.O. 12106.
PRINCIPAL PURPOSE:	Formal filing of allegation of discrimination because of race, color, religion, sex, disability, age, national origin or reprisal.
ROUTINE USES:	Information in this system may be disclosed to Federal, State or local investigating agencies, the Congress when inquiring on behalf of the individual; to any official engaged in the investigation of settlement of matters at issue; to the EEOC as necessary; and to another Federal agency or court in compliance with a subpoena.
DISCLOSURE:	Voluntary; however, failure to complete all appropriate portions of this form may lead to dismissal of complaint on the basis of inadequate data on which to determine if complaint is acceptable. EEOC government-wide system notices EEOC/GOVT-1 applied.

1. NAME OF COMPLAINANT (Last, First, Middle Initial)

Social Security Number: -   -

2. AGENCY DOCKET/COMPLAINT NO. (EEO OFFICE USE ONLY)

3a. HOME PHONE NUMBER	**3b. WORK PHONE NUMBER**	**4. HOME ADDRESS** (Include city, state & zip code)

5. DO YOU HAVE A REPRESENTATIVE?
☐ a. YES (Complete Item 6)   ☐ b. NO

6. IF YES, PROVIDE NAME, ADDRESS & PHONE NUMBER OF REPRESENTATIVE (Include city, state, & zip code)

IS YOUR REPRESENTATIVE AN ATTORNEY? ☐ YES ☐ NO

7. NAME OF AGENCY & ADDRESS WHERE ALLEGATIONS AROSE (Include city, state, & zip code)

8. NAME & LOCATION OF AGENCY ORGANIZATION WHERE YOU WORK	**9. DATE OF MOST RECENT ACT OF ALLEGED DISCRIMINATION (MMDDYY)**	**10. ARE YOU A FEDERAL EMPLOYEE OR APPLICANT?**
		☐ a. EMPLOYEE: GRADE, SERIES, TITLE
		☐ b. APPLICANT

11. REASON YOU BELIEVE YOU WERE DISCRIMINATED AGAINST ("X" BELOW)

a. RACE (If so, state your Race)	**e. DISABILITY** (Describe nature of your disability) ☐ Physical: ☐ Mental:
b. COLOR (If so, state your Color)	**f. AGE** (If so, state your date of birth) [Applies to persons at least 40 years of age at the time of alleged discriminatory action.]
c. RELIGION (If so, state your Religion)	**g. SEX** (If so, state your gender)
d. NATIONAL ORIGIN (If so, state your Natural Origin)	**h. REPRISAL** (Provide date and nature of your participation in an EEO-protected activity or opposition to discrimination practices.)

12. I HAVE DISCUSSED MY COMPLAINT WITH AN EEO COUNSELOR ☐ a. YES (Complete 12c) ☐ b. NO	**12c. IF "YES," NAME & PHONE NUMBER OF COUNSELOR**	**12d. DATE YOU FIRST ASKED TO SEE AN EEO COUNSELOR**	**13. DATE RECEIVED NOTICE OF FINAL INTERVIEW/RIGHT TO FILE**

14. TELL BRIEFLY HOW YOU WERE DISCRIMINATED AGAINST; INCLUDE THE DATE OF EACH ALLEGED DISCRIMINATORY INCIDENT.
(That is, tell how you were treated differently from other employees or applicants because of your race, color, religion, sex, national origin, age, mental or physical disability or reprisal.)

15. WHAT SPECIFIC CORRECTIVE ACTION DO YOU WANT TAKEN ON YOUR COMPLAINT? (If more than one allegation is being made, state overall corrective action desired and the specific correct action desired for each separate allegation.)

16. HAVE ANY OF THE INCIDEENTS LISTED IN ITEM 14 BEEN APPEALED TO THE MERIT SYSTEMS PROTECTION BOARD (MSPB) OR FILED UNDER A NEGOTIATED GRIEVANCE PROCEDURE? ☐ a. YES. Explain. (Include data and MSPB Docket No.) ☐ b. NO	**17. SIGNATURE OF COMPLAINANT**
	18. DATE OF COMPLAINT SIGNED BY COMPLAINANT (MMDDYY) / **19. DATE COMPLAINT FILED (EEO OFFICE USE ONLY)**

However, keep in mind that you don't always have to file your formal complaint on one of these forms. Unless the agency specifically requires you to do so, you can feel free to simply write a letter to the appropriate person lodging your formal complaint. At the end of this chapter, you will find a sample of a complaint letter we wrote for a client alleging discrimination against the U.S. Army Corps of Engineers.

That being said, using the form provided by your agency will help in the processing of your formal complaint. Interestingly, in most cases, due to space constraints, you will need to also attach an explanatory letter to the agency form, which usually doesn't have enough room to hold a full description of your allegations. On the next page, you will find a sample complaint form.

Remember, you should address this form/letter to the person indicated in the Notice of Right to File a Formal Complaint. As discussed in the previous chapter, you should receive this notice from your EEO Counselor in your final interview. If by some chance you don't receive this notice in your final interview, or the counselor is dragging his or her feet and you want to move the process along, you can get this information by visiting your agency's EEO office or the office that handles personnel issues.

Also, you should be very careful when filling out any agency form, because some of them are tricky. For example, one form we encountered lists "sexual orientation" as a basis that you can check for discrimination. This is despite the fact that, as we explained earlier, sexual orientation is <u>not</u> a protected basis under Title VII and is not a basis of discrimination enforced by the EEOC. As a result, if you are experiencing "gender stereotyping" and check this box by mistake, your case could be dismissed, regardless of the fact that you had a perfectly valid claim under Title VII for gender discrimination. Sadly, this has happened to some federal employees. Likewise, some forms list other invalid bases for EEO discrimination claims, such as "marital status" or "political affiliation." If you check one of these boxes, it could be fatal to your case. Once again, be careful when filling out an agency-supplied form.

Complaint Requirements

In filling out your complaint form, or in writing a complaint letter, there are a few specific requirements you should be sure to include.

Signatures and Contact Information

Your formal complaint must be signed by you, or if you've retained counsel, by your lawyer. Furthermore, your complaint must contain a telephone number and address at which you (or your attorney) can be reached. It's important to remember that you must notify the agency of any change in your contact information if you should move or change phone numbers at any time during the processing of your complaint.

Timely Filing

Make sure to mention the most recent date of discrimination and the date of your *initial* contact with your counselor to demonstrate that you've met the 45-day requirement. You might also want to mention if it is a continuing violation, especially in matters involving a hostile work environment, a "pattern and practice" allegation, or a class action covering a few years of illegal policies.

Specific Grounds for Discrimination

Most importantly, in your formal complaint, you must state the **specific grounds** for your claim of unlawful discrimination. It isn't enough to write that you've been the victim of discrimination. You must demonstrate that your rights have been violated under one or more of the four laws we already discussed (Title VII, ADEA, Rehabilitation Act/ADA, or EPA) and you must give enough information to support your claim.

At a minimum, you must explain the basis of the discrimination, how it was committed, by whom and when. In short, what you're trying to do is to make a strong enough case so that the person reading your letter can say, "Assuming that everything in this letter is true, the complainant has a valid case for discrimination."

This is vitally important because, if you fail to adequately state your claim of unlawful discrimination, the agency can dismiss your complaint outright. You'll want to provide enough facts so that this doesn't happen. On the other hand, you don't want to write a book on the subject. The key is to provide all of the pertinent information but none of the extraneous information, regardless of how "juicy" it might be.

Of course, this is easier said than done. Yet, it shouldn't be too difficult if you keep in mind the bases for unlawful discrimination that were discussed in Chapter 1. As you remember, in that chapter, we discussed the four statutes defining unlawful discrimination in EEOC actions. In your formal complaint, your goal should be to simply demonstrate how your employer violated one or more of these laws.

To illustrate, we'll give you examples of how you might go about writing your formal complaint in each situation. Of course, these are just examples and you'll have to modify them to meet your purposes.

Title VII

As you remember, Title VII prohibits your employer from discriminating against you in hiring, promotion or other employment opportunities on the basis of your race, color, religion, gender or national origin. Yet, it's not enough to simply write in your formal complaint that you are a member of a racial or religious minority or that you are a woman and you have been the victim of discrimination. You must explain the discrimination in detail – how it happened, when it happened, where it happened and by whom.

Demonstrating Discrimination Though Overt Actions

Let's start with an example of racial discrimination. For this purpose, let's suppose that you're an African American, and you believe that you were passed over for a promotion because of your race (and a Caucasian or Hispanic or Asian was selected). In your letter, you must explain *why* you think *race* was a factor, or was *the* factor, in the selection process. If your belief is based on the fact that your immediate supervisor has been known to make racist comments, then you must explain this fact in your letter. You should explain the exact nature of those comments and give enough detail to support your accusation.

For example, writing in your letter that "everyone knows that Mr. Smith is a racist" is far less persuasive than writing, "On June 22nd of this year, I overheard Mr. Smith having a conversation with Ms. Jones in which Mr. Smith said, 'I just can't stand the thought of all of these black people getting ahead in the agency. I'll tell you one thing. I'll never promote one if I have any choice in the matter.'"

This latter description is superior in two ways. For one, it provides direct evidence of bias that can be investigated. At the very least, the EEO Investigator can speak with Ms. Jones to corroborate your claim. Second, you have not only demonstrated a bias, but you've also demonstrated how that bias resulted in a violation of your Title VII rights.

Claims of other forms of bias (religious, national origin, gender and color) should be expressed in a similar fashion. You want to demonstrate your case with specific allegations of discrimination. Of course, you won't always have a situation where your boss has acted in such a blatantly discriminatory manner. In fact, in most cases, the discrimination will be rather subtle.

However, you can still make specific allegations of discrimination by way of comparison.

Demonstrating Discrimination by Comparison

For example, let's suppose that you're a person of the Islamic faith while your boss is a Christian. As far as you know, your boss has never expressed hostility towards Muslims, but you've sensed it; particularly when it comes to religious observances. Your Christian colleagues regularly receive allowances for religious observances while your requests are usually denied. In this case, you should include this information in your complaint letter.

Once again, it helps to be as specific as possible. A statement like "Ms. Williams is much nicer to Christians than Muslims" is of limited value to the investigator. On the other hand, if you include specific instances (including dates and times) when you've been treated differently than someone of a different religious faith, you greatly diminish the chances of having your complaint dismissed. You also provide a way for the investigator to confirm the accuracy of your claims.

You can use a similar strategy if you've been discriminated against in getting a promotion on the basis of your race or some other unlawful basis. For instance, let's suppose you're a Hispanic woman who has been passed over a promotion, despite you're being objectively the most logical pick for the position. Instead, your boss, a white female, promoted another white female to the position. In this case, you can bolster your claim for discrimination if you can provide concrete evidence that you were the most qualified candidate. This means that if you have more seniority and a near perfect history of reviews, you should say so. Sure, you may not have access to the other person's employment file, but if you have reason to believe that your past performance is at least comparable to her past performance, then, once again, put it in your complaint.

Religious Compensatory Time

Some types of discrimination under Title VII do not require comparison, like "reasonable accommodation" for religious observances. A federal employee who has a sincere religious belief that requires him or her to abstain from work is allowed to use "Religious Compensatory Time," and to earn RCT outside of their normal 40 hour tour of duty, barring a showing by the agency of "undue hardship." The EEOC has issued many favorable decisions on this issue and, since there is no need to show intentional discrimination in such cases, they can be relatively easy to win.

Demonstrating Disparate Impact

Now, in some cases, the discrimination may be so subtle that it simply defies description. You can't point to anything specific but somehow, it seems that a certain *class* of people in your workplace never seems to get promotions, training opportunities and the like. In the law, this type of discrimination is called "disparate impact" discrimination. The policies of the workplace may not be intentionally discriminatory, but their *impact* on certain groups creates disparate results.

If you believe that this is the case in your workplace, then that's what you should state in your formal complaint. You don't need to necessarily "prove" your case for disparate impact in your complaint, but at least you do need to make the argument.

And once again, a specific argument is much better than a generic argument. For instance, it might not be enough to write, "In my office, women just never seem to get ahead." In this case, it would be much better to be able to write, "Of the last six promotions to supervisor, all six of them went to men, despite the fact that two-thirds of the employees in my department are women." If you know that two-thirds of the applicants for promotion have consistently been women, then you should state that fact as well.

By the way, don't be intimidated if you don't have specific numbers to support your claim. You're not expected to rummage through the personnel files in the office to make your case. Later, the investigator can determine exactly how many promotions there have been in the office and exactly what percentage of the workforce is female. The important thing is to make a specific and credible allegation of disparate impact so that there is something for the investigator to follow up on.

Demonstrating Sexual Harassment

Also, as you recall, sexual harassment claims are covered under Title VII. If you've been the victim of sexual harassment, then it's important to provide specific allegations of unlawful conduct in your letter. For example, if you've been subjected to *quid pro quo* sexual discrimination, then explain *exactly* what happened. Simply writing that your boss "kept hitting on me" is not nearly as helpful as writing, "On April 23rd of this year, Ms. Baker put her hands on my leg and said, 'You know, if you learn how to please the boss, you can go places in this department. How about joining me for a drink at my place tonight?'"

It's also important in this context to explain how you reacted to these advances. If you told your boss that her advances were unwelcome, say so.

And if you didn't say anything to your boss, but politely declined for fear of retribution, also say so. This is particularly important in the case in which you felt so much pressure that you succumbed to your boss's demands. You want to get it on the record early that you're acquiescence wasn't voluntary.

You should be equally specific in hostile workplace claims. It's not enough to write "The atmosphere on the factory floor was hostile to women." Instead, you will want to give as many concrete examples as possible. "On November 12th of this year, Jimmy Patterson grabbed my buttocks and said, 'You know you like it, baby!'" We realize that it might be uncomfortable to give specific details, but they're going to have to come out sooner or later and it's better to reveal them on your own terms.

You should also name witnesses to incidents, if any. After all, favorable affidavits from witnesses supporting your version of the events can go a long way towards helping you resolve the case early. Besides, it's better to know early on which witnesses will support you (and which won't).

Also, you will need to demonstrate that you went to someone for help, but didn't receive any assistance. Therefore, it will be important to explain, in detail, whom you spoke to, what they said (or didn't say), and how the conduct continued anyway.

As always, the more facts you can demonstrate in support of your case, the better chance you have of keeping your complaint from being dismissed. This is particularly important in the context of a hostile work environment.

Other Claims of Hostile Work Environment

In many cases, to prove a hostile work environment, you need to illustrate that the actions of your co-workers were either outrageous or persistent. One isolated off-color joke or one inappropriate comment may not be enough to show that you've been subjected to a "severe" or "pervasive" hostile work environment. Therefore, if you've been subjected to *numerous* cases of inappropriate behavior, list as many of them as you can remember. And if possible, provide as many dates, times, locations and witness names as possible.

And even if you can't remember the exact date and time, try to estimate it. For example, if you remember that the incident took place sometime just before Christmas, write something like, "Sometime around the middle of December...." Obviously, a contemporaneous diary would be great evidence in such a case; since the environment might not get any better (or might even get worse), consider starting a diary right away and filling in a timeline as far back as you can go. One of our hostile work environment cases prevailed in part because the client kept a detailed daily diary and backed it up with emails and witnesses, all of which combined to corroborate her testimony and credibility.

Once again, the point is to provide enough information to get the ball rolling for the investigator. Remember, the more examples of discrimination you can provide (and the more specific you can be in making those allegations), the more likely it is that your complaint will survive the early stage of the process and avoid being dismissed for failure to state a claim.

ADEA

The Age Discrimination in Employment Act protects individuals who are 40 or older from workplace discrimination. If you've been the victim of age discrimination, then you should state so in your formal complaint. And, once again, you should lay out all of the facts necessary to support your assertion.

Remember, being 40 or older doesn't make you immune from being passed over for promotion, cut out of overtime opportunities, coerced into resigning, being fired, laid off, demoted or denied training opportunities. These things can happen to any employee, regardless of age. The ADEA only protects you from being subjected to these circumstances *because* of your age. Therefore, under the ADEA, your employer can't make the decision that since you are say, 50 years old, you won't be allowed to participate in management training because you're just going to retire soon anyway.

This being the case, your complaint letter should not only explain what adverse actions have been taken against you, but that those actions were the result of your age. Once again, the key is to be as specific as possible. If your boss has made specific comments about his bias towards older workers, then put these down in your letter. And remember to include the precise nature of the comment, when it was made, where it was made and who was around to hear it.

Likewise, if you've lost out on an employment opportunity to a younger co-worker simply on the basis of your age, demonstrate in your letter that this was the case. If you have a superior work record or test results, indicate so in your letter. Also, please note that the ADEA protects you in this case even if the younger worker also happens to be over 40. Therefore, if you're, say, 62, and your co-worker is 42, you can still the victim of unlawful age discrimination.

Finally, the disparate impact analysis is also available in age discrimination cases. Many employers attempt to reduce costs by laying off experienced higher-paid workers and replacing them with inexperienced lower-paid younger workers. In many cases, this decision isn't based on an animus or bias toward older workers, but simply a desire to cut costs. Yet, this unbiased decision does have a disparate impact on older workers as they are more likely to be the victims of this strategy.

If you've been the victim of such "young-sizing," then say so in your complaint letter. And support your case with as many facts as possible. If you can point out, say, that over a six-month period, 70% of the workers laid off were 40 or older and that 90% of these workers were replaced by workers under 40 years of age, your case is that much stronger. As with Title VII allegations, specific allegations in an ADEA context are better than general allegations.

Rehabilitation Act/Americans with Disabilities Act

The Rehabilitation Act and its private sector counterpart (whose standards now apply to all Rehab Act cases), the Americans with Disabilities Act, protect workers from being discriminated against on the basis of a disability. Furthermore, under the Rehab Act/ADA, employers are required to make "reasonable accommodation" to accommodate those with disabilities.

If you feel that you have been discriminated against because of a disability or that your employer hasn't made reasonable accommodation in your case, then your complaint letter should reflect those facts.

As always, it's important to be specific as possible in making these claims. In most cases, the issue will be one of "reasonable accommodation." In explaining your case, you should obviously explain your disability. In doing so, you should show that you meet the definition of being disabled, which, for purposes of the ADA, is the substantial impairment of a major life activity.

Second, you should demonstrate that, while you are disabled, you can perform the essential functions of the job if your employer would only make a reasonable accommodation. Furthermore, you should detail your attempts to get your employer to make such an accommodation. In doing so, you should mention any attempts your employer did make in this regard and explain why they weren't reasonable in relation to your condition.

Once again, the point here is to demonstrate enough facts so that, if true, the EEOC would rule in your favor. While this level of detail may not be strictly necessary, you don't want to give the agency an opportunity to dismiss your complaint before you've had an opportunity to have a full-scale investigation.

Another type of disability discrimination encountered frequently is when an employee is not really disabled, but their employer "perceives" them to be disabled. Sometimes an agency says that you cannot do your job, but you can. That is also disability discrimination.

Often we see other forms of violation of the Rehab Act, such as sharing of confidential medical information, or inquiries about medical conditions from one's supervisor when they have no need to know, or questions about medical conditions in a job interview. All of these can be considered illegal discrimination under the Rehab Act.

Hostile work environments exist for disabled employees as well as others. We won a case for an employee who had a severe limp due to a foot and leg disability and who was repeatedly called "Gimpy," "Hopalong," "Chester" (an apparent reference to a Western TV character with a peg leg), and whose spiral shaped cane was stroked by co-workers and supervisors and called "Snakey." The client was also challenged to a wheelchair race, during – of all times of the year – Disability Sensitivity Month.

EPA

The Equal Pay Act of 1963 prevents employers from paying employees of one gender more than employees of another gender to perform the same job. Thus, men as well as women may sue for illegal discrimination if they are being paid less than the opposite gender for the same work. Importantly, it must be substantially the same work performed substantially the same way. An expert witness is very helpful, in our experience, to prove this type of claim.

Therefore, if you file a complaint on EPA grounds, at the very least, you should specifically demonstrate that someone of the *opposite* gender is making more money to perform your same job. However, that, by itself, is not enough. Employers are entitled to pay different amounts to different workers depending upon seniority or the quality or quantity of production. For instance, a male employee with 30 years of service can be lawfully paid more than a female employer with 3 years of service. Likewise, a male salesperson can be paid far in excess of his female counterpart if he makes more sales. As a result, it isn't only important to demonstrate a pay disparity, but also to explain that there is no logical or economic reason for the disparity.

Now, please understand that you don't have to "prove" your case at this time. After all, it may require expert witness testimony to determine that there is no need for a difference in pay. That can take place during the investigation, or more likely, during the hearing or at trial. However, for now, it makes sense to at least attempt to address the issue of the pay differential so that your claim isn't immediately dismissed as just a misinterpretation of the law.

Importantly, a desk audit is much different than an EPA claim. If you request a desk audit, the agency has the right to actually downgrade you. In an EPA claim, your grade does not matter and you are not supposed to be audited – the classification of your job is not at issue, but rather your work is supposed to be compared to the job duties of the different-gender comparator you have chosen. They are not supposed to be adversely affected either.

SAMPLE COMPLAINT LETTER

Ms. Marie Bobblehead
EEO Officer
P.O. Box 1715
Somewhere, DC 20202

>   Re: **Complaint of Discrimination**
>   **Complainant v. U.S. Army Corps of Engineers**

Dear Ms. Bobblehead:

Please allow this letter to serve as my complaint of discrimination against the U.S. Army Corps of Engineers. I have contacted your office both by phone and in person and have received no response. Most recently, on December 16, 2004, I came to your office to file a complaint of discrimination and filled out an Information Inquiry Summary. Since that date, I have received no further communication from your office. I have therefore sought timely counseling but no EEO counselor has contacted me. Thirty days have passed and this is a Formal Complaint of Discrimination.

My complaint of discrimination includes the following:

- I am a 51 year old Asian female and I began working for United States Corps of Engineers in 1990-1991 as a Procurement Technician, GS-5. As of today, I am still in the same position.

- There are 6 Procurement Technicians with same series and title. Every one of them, including 4 Caucasian females, is a GS-7 except for me. We all have the exact same job title, and have at times performed similar work. Yet, I have remained as a GS-5.

- I requested a desk audit at the same time as a Caucasian worker for the same work; she was promoted but I was not.

- I have requested, on a continuous basis, Flexiplace/work at home. I have been denied and a Caucasian co-worker was approved but it is not clear what, if any, work she does at home.

- Management has intentionally given the Caucasian employees better work assignments in order to promote them.

- I feel that I am being discriminated based on my race and age by management because I have been treated differently than other, Caucasian, Procurement Technicians.

- Secondly, I have been treated differently than other employees in that I have received a lower rating than all of the other employees. My lowered ratings are also discriminatory in nature. This has meant that I do not receive any monetary awards.

- I have also been subject to harassment and a hostile work environment by my supervisors including Mr. Harasser, Assistant Chief of Procurement. He told me on several occasions that I should not speak to other supervisors about any problems I am having. He told me that he put my name on a list of people who were going to retire without having received my permission.

- Dr. Hostile, Chief of Procurement, told me to go find a job somewhere else. His actions were discrimination based on my age and race. Dr. Rich also said that I would be sitting here in 10 years complaining about the same thing. These discriminatory remarks and the constant and severe harassment by my supervisors have lead to a hostile work environment.

- Lastly, on December 6, 2004, I was given a memorandum of counseling by Mr. Uptonogood, which was unfair and discriminatory in nature. When Mr. Uptonogood became my supervisor in November 2004, he interviewed me and cancelled my credit card which I had used for purchasing. No other employee had their credit card taken from them. Mr. Uptonogood then asked me to work on supplies and repeatedly harassed me regarding status reports. No other employees were subject to this behavior. I was then unfairly accused of not working fast enough.

- In short, I am being subjected to disparate treatment and a hostile work environment based upon illegal factors such as my race.

Please be aware that I am being represented by counsel in the above referenced matter. After reviewing the Complaint of Discrimination, please contact my attorney so the appropriate actions can be taken.

Sincerely,

_____   _____
Complainant   Date

_____
Snider & Associates, LLC
1-800-DISCRIMINATION
"Justice in the Workplace"

Enclosures

Chapter 10

The Investigation

In this chapter, we'll explain what *should* happen during the 180-day investigation period after you file your formal complaint. In a perfect world, all of the following rules and procedures would be followed to the letter. As you know, we don't live in such a world and therefore, the process may not proceed as designed. For this reason, it's important that you understand your rights.

By knowing your rights, you have the opportunity to correct any mistakes that occur during the process. For example, at the end of the investigation, the EEO Investigator must provide you with an opportunity to examine the investigative file and address any deficiencies in it. In the best case scenario, the investigator should then take action to correct any deficiencies. At worst, your letter setting forth the deficiencies should be included in the investigative file to be reviewed by the agency, or the administrative judge, if you later decide to go to a hearing.

Sadly, some investigators must be "reminded" of their responsibility to allow you to examine the investigative file. This is why it's so important that you thoroughly understand how the process is *supposed* to work. It's also important because procedural irregularities can be used to demonstrate that the investigative process (and the resulting agency determination) was flawed.

For example, according to EEOC policy, investigators must be unbiased and objective. To ensure the objectivity of its investigators, the EEOC has established certain rules. One of these rules is that the investigator shall not occupy a position in the agency that is directly or indirectly under the jurisdiction of the head of that part of the agency in which the complaint arose. If this occurs in your situation, then it could be helpful to explain this conflict of interest when later challenging an adverse agency determination. However, in most cases, it will be up to you to make this fact known and you will only know to do so by having an in-depth knowledge of the proper procedure for the investigation process.

The Acknowledgment Letter

As soon as the agency receives your complaint, it should send you a letter acknowledging that it has received the complaint. This letter is fairly boilerplate and won't contain any findings on the part of the agency. However, the letter will state your official filing date of the complaint. This date will be used in establishing the 180-day period in which the agency has to take action on your complaint. As we explained before, if you mail your complaint, the filing date will be the date of the postmark and not the date that the complaint was actually received by the agency.

The Acceptance Letter

Sometime after receiving the Acknowledgment Letter, the agency will send you a second letter. This letter is commonly referred to as the "acceptance letter." The acceptance letter states the claims that will be investigated by the agency during the 180-day period. Hopefully, the agency will agree to investigate *all* of the claims presented in your formal complaint. Yet, this may not be the case. The agency may decide to dismiss one or more of your claims for a variety of reasons.

As we discussed at length in the last chapter, if you fail to state a claim that alleges discrimination based on one of the required grounds (e.g., race, religion, gender, age, etc.) or you fail to allege facts that, if true, would constitute unlawful discrimination, your complaint may be dismissed. In other words, the agency will usually dismiss any claims for which you do not have a case.

Also, the agency will usually dismiss your claim if you didn't contact an EEO Counselor within 45 days of the discriminatory event, unless there were extenuating circumstances to explain your delay. Amazingly, in some cases, the agency will miss this timing issue and won't raise it until later in the case; perhaps, not until the administrative hearing. For this reason, you should always be fully prepared to explain any delay at the first available opportunity. This same advice applies to the 15-day deadline for filing the formal complaint.

Finally, the agency may dismiss your claim if you have raised the same claim in a negotiated grievance proceeding or before the Merit System Protection Board. Likewise, your claim may be dismissed if you've already brought this claim in a previous complaint or if the issue is moot. The most common other reason for initial dismissal is the lack of the tangible employment action. As we discussed earlier, discrimination must have some tangible component to it. Claims that can be typically dismissed on this basis include failure to get into a training course and placement on a 120-day detail (unless supported by tangible evidence of loss to the employee).

Unfortunately, there may be no immediate appeal of a dismissal of one of your claims by the agency. If your *entire* claim is dismissed, you can appeal that to the EEOC's Office of Federal Operations ("OFO"). Many cases are remanded for investigation by the OFO, so don't give up if this happens to you. If, however, only *some* of your claims are dismissed, then you must wait until your administrative hearing or your appeal from final agency action before you can challenge the dismissal. However, in the meantime, you can (and should) submit a statement to the agency concerning its dismissal of the claim and why you believe it is incorrect. This statement can become part of the complaint file, or the factual record.

The Investigation

During the investigative part of the proceeding, most of your energies should be focused on building a factual record that supports your claim of discrimination. After all, if your complaint reaches the hearing stage, the administrative judge is going to review the factual record to get a feel for the case. Some EEOC Hearings offices (where the administrative judges are stationed) use a "triage" system where cases are dismissed or set for an expedited docket or for summary judgment briefs immediately, based solely upon what is contained in the investigative report, often called the "Report of Investigation" ("ROI"). Needless to say, the stronger your claim looks in the file, the better chance you have of getting the judge to take your case seriously and allow you the latitude to gather further information during the discovery phase of the hearing.

Of course, you won't be in charge of compiling the factual record. That responsibility falls to the EEO Investigator. The investigator is a person officially authorized to conduct inquiries into claims raised in EEO complaints. In this capacity, the investigator has the power to administer oaths and compel employees to testify under oath.

The purpose of the investigation is two-fold. First, the investigator is attempting to gather facts that would allow a reasonable person to draw a conclusion as to whether you have been subjected to unlawful discrimination. Second, if unlawful discrimination is found, the factual record should be helpful in fashioning a suitable remedy.

Your Affidavit

The initial step in the investigative process will be for the investigator to review your complaint. If the investigator requires additional information or clarification, he or she may call you in for an interview. The investigator may record this interview or simply make handwritten notes of the conversation.

In other cases, the investigator may send you written questions (interrogatories) or simply ask you to further explain the discrimination in writing. Many investigators type up your statement in affidavit form and have you sign it. Other investigators, like those at the Office of Complaint Investigations at the Department of Defense (DOD), may conduct a full blown evidentiary hearing proceeding, with live testimony and a court reporter. Nevertheless, this is not the most common method of performing investigations.

Be very careful in writing, editing and signing your affidavit. This is going to be the basis for all further decision-making on your case. It is the first thing that most people reviewing the ROI are going to read. Make sure that it is factual, grounded in definite time frames and cites corroborating evidence, like what other witnesses exist, what documents support your claims, etc.

You can attach to your affidavit documents that support the complaint and provide in the affidavit names of witnesses that you would like the investigator to interview.

Witness Affidavits, Collecting of Documents

The investigator is supposed to interview, whether in person or through written questions and answers, other witnesses that might have information related to your complaint, including the person(s) named in your complaint as discriminating officials, also called Responsible Management Official(s) (RMOs). Also, the investigator is supposed to obtain all relevant documents, such as personnel files and agency policies. Finally, if statistical information is needed to determine a claim of disparate impact, the investigator is supposed to obtain this information from the EEO or other sources.

Unfortunately, EEO Investigators, who are usually contractors conducting the investigation on a flat-fee basis, often fail to perform a full and fair investigation. They sometimes (perhaps often) don't interview key witnesses, fail to ask the right questions and don't ask for, or push for, important documents. You can help the investigator by naming the witnesses who will confirm your version of the events and providing their addresses and phone numbers. You should also give the investigator a detailed description of what the witnesses know and/or will testify to.

Sadly, you may have to educate the investigator about what types of agency documents he or she should be looking for. Finally, whenever you supply the investigator with information, you should do so in writing so that it can be made part of the ROI.

What to do if the Investigation Takes Too Long

As you can imagine, the investigative process can be a slow-moving process. This 180-day period can feel like a lifetime. Yet, the good news is that it is a strictly observed time period. If the investigator has not completed the ROI and delivered it to you within 180 days, you are free to take the next step. In fact, as early as the 181st day, you should feel free to request a hearing (as our firm has done on a number of occasions for clients in situations where the agency failed to timely finish, or on occasion, even start the investigation).

In some cases, the agency will ask you to agree to a one-time 90-day extension. Please keep in mind that you don't have to agree to such a request. You can hold the agency to the 180-day time limit, unless you are the reason for the delay for failing to timely respond to requests for information from the investigator.

Needless to say, this is something you should avoid at all costs. Not only will you needlessly delay the process, but you run the risk of having your complaint dismissed on this ground. This is despite the fact that the agency will rarely suffer such adverse consequences for being tardy in its responsibilities.

Amending Your Complaint

In the meantime, keep in mind that you should feel free to update the investigator as to any new developments affecting your claim. Once again, always do so in writing. As we discussed earlier, in some cases, employees suffer retaliation at the hands of those whom they file complaints against. In other cases, new information may become available to you as colleagues or other persons share information with you that is relevant to your claim.

If you have a new matter or incident that is not included in your initial complaint, but is similar or related to the matters raised in the complaint, you can include these matters by amending your complaint at any time prior to end of the investigation period. This is preferred to filing a new complaint. And please note that you can not amend your charge by simply informing the investigator. Instead, you must address a formal letter to the Director (or equivalent) of Equal Opportunity at your agency, and if the additional issue is accepted, the investigator will be informed via letter from that office.

Of course, the new claims in your complaint must be *like or related to* the original claims. For this purpose, claims of retaliation or further discrimination on the same basis are like or related to the original claim. For instance, if your original complaint claims that your co-workers are harassing you on the basis of your gender, then any future instances of harassment by these co-workers will usually be the proper subject of an amended complaint. The same is true if you're the victim of retaliation or another discriminatory action, like being denied a promotion.

However, let's take the case of an African-American woman who has been denied job training opportunities by her supervisor. She believes this denial was made on the basis of gender and has filed a formal complaint. During the 180-day investigation, she attempts to get a job with another federal agency, but is denied on the basis of her race. In this case, her claim of racial discrimination involving a different agency is <u>not related</u> to her claim of gender discrimination involving her current employer. This claim should be the subject of an entirely different EEO investigation, requiring the complainant to contact the EEO Counselor at the other agency and begin the counseling process anew on that claim.

Supplementing the ROI

Also, during the investigative period, it's important to keep the EEO Investigator abreast of any changes in your address or telephone numbers. Your complaint may be dismissed in its entirety if the investigator is unable to contact you for additional information because you have moved or changed telephone numbers.

An important, and virtually unknown, fact is that *any document* included in the ROI is deemed "admitted" at any hearing before an administrative judge (AJ). This will be explained further in future chapters on the hearing, but keep in mind that you can fill the ROI with all of your evidence and it will be "in evidence" before the hearing even starts, making your job much easier at the hearing stage.

Finally, remember to keep multiple paper copies of all important documents. Originals can get lost, misplaced or destroyed and if key evidence is missing, you may not be able to prove that a meeting took place or that you told someone something important. With email as prolific as it is, you will want to print out and keep copies of anything that is remotely related to your claim, just in case you need it for your case.

Rebuttal Affidavit

After the investigator takes your statement or affidavit, and that of the RMO(s), your witnesses and agency witnesses, you are usually given an opportunity to view the agency witnesses' affidavits and offer a rebuttal affidavit. Don't pass up this golden opportunity to explain your case *again* and point out the inconsistencies in the agency's explanation. Also, take this opportunity to provide plentiful documentary evidence as an attachment to your supplemental affidavit or statement, to be included in the record. If you need an extension to get information to the investigator, ask for it, and do so in writing.

Also note in your rebuttal affidavit what evidence the Investigator *could* have collected but did not collect. You could request (and receive) sanctions against the agency for its failure to conduct a complete and thorough investigation. Therefore, at this stage, identify what witnesses *could* have been interviewed (and why they are important to have been interviewed), what they would have said, what documents *should* have been collected but were not, etc. With any luck, the investigator will request those documents and interview those witnesses. But also beware that some investigators will go back to management after you have given your rebuttal affidavit – and offer them a chance to offer their own rebuttal affidavit to yours! We have even experienced an investigator who created an entire supplemental ROI just to try and prove a client wrong. It doesn't help when the investigator is biased, gets to choose who to interview, and also gets to choose what questions to ask.

Chapter 11

Choosing a Decision Maker

The investigative stage of the process ends when you receive a copy of the ROI. This file will contain a copy of the EEO Counselor's Report, Notice of Final Interview, the Formal Complaint and any amendments to the complaint. It will also contain a copy of the acceptance letter and copies of all evidence collected by the investigator. The file also includes the investigator's summary of the investigation, which will state the issues and delineate the evidence addressing both sides of each issue in the matter.

Note that the investigation summary will not usually come to any definitive conclusions about the merit of your claim. In other words, the role of the investigator is to simply investigate your claims. He or she is not supposed to, and usually does not, make a decision or even voice an opinion about the merits of your case. In fact, at this stage in the process, no decision has been made by anyone. This decision is to be made in the next stage of the process – the adjudicative stage.

However, in many agencies, the paid contract investigator is ordered to provide an opinion. In other cases, the ROI is given to the agency to "clean up" (i.e., someone will edit the investigator's report to help their position as much as possible). All too often, a conclusion of "Finding: No Discrimination" is added to the ROI.

Thankfully, this opinion is given very little weight by the administrative judge. Yet, it often dissuades employees with a good case from going forward. Obviously, our advice is to *ignore* the agency's bogus findings and seek an expert opinion on your case before abandoning it.

As you probably remember, you have three options at the end of the investigation (or after 180 days from filing your complaint if the investigation has not been completed by then). First, you can ask the agency to make a final determination about your claim. Second, you can request a hearing before an administrative judge. Third, you can file a lawsuit in federal court.

With three different options, how do you decide? Well, fortunately (or perhaps, unfortunately), you really only have two viable options, as your chances of winning the case on a final agency determination are next to nil. Therefore, your real options are between the administrative hearing and a lawsuit.

Of course, if you have the financial resources to bring back-to-back actions, then you could always pursue the hearing and, if that fails, bring a federal lawsuit afterwards. However, if your financial situation affords you only one opportunity to litigate your case, you should strongly consider the following factors: (1) the availability of witnesses; (2) the informal nature of an administrative hearing; and (3) the jury appeal of your case.

Availability of Witnesses

There is no subpoena power (currently) for EEOC Administrative Judges. They can, however, compel some people to testify. The only witnesses who can be compelled to testify are: (1) *current* employees of your agency; (2) former employees of your agency who now work for another federal agency (with a few exceptions, like for employees of the Library of Congress); and (3) any executive branch employee, regardless of their location. In contrast, in federal court, your attorney can issue a subpoena for virtually anyone to appear at a deposition or at trial, depending on geographic location. Needless to say, this advantage of being able to compel anyone's presence at a deposition or trial can be critical.

For instance, we once had a case that came down to interpretation of a union contract. Our client wanted to compel the testimony of a union president, who was a postal employee on permanent leave without pay status. At the administrative hearing, the judge ruled that the union president was a "private citizen" and, as such, beyond the power of the administrative judge to order his presence. Unfortunately for us, the union president's testimony was critical to disprove the testimony of the management official who, in our view, had discriminated against our client. As a result, once the judge issued this ruling, we immediately advised our client to drop his case at the administrative level and move to federal court, where the union president's attendance could be secured easily.

Informal Nature of Administrative Hearings

By nature, administrative hearings are much more informal than court proceedings. You can represent yourself much more easily, and you can be represented by a non-attorney representative before the EEOC. In court, you will either be on your own (pro se) or you will need a lawyer.

Administrative judges are allowed to listen to hearsay, which is not allowed in court. Many fewer cases are dismissed on summary judgment before the EEOC than in US District Court, and the cases can move quicker before an administrative judge.

AJs are also experts in their field. EEO hearings are all they do, so they are very familiar with the burdens of proof and are sensitive (as federal employees themselves) to the rights of complainants. On the other hand, U.S. District Court Judges have an already overloaded docket of criminal cases, including many drug cases, white collar cases and business law cases, and are notoriously disinterested in hearing employment law matters.

These are some reasons that may lead you to conclude that an administrative hearing is better for your case than heading to federal court.

Jury Appeal

The jury appeal of a case can have a significant impact on the decision to bring a lawsuit in federal court. That being said, it's important to point out that not all cases brought in federal court go to a jury. The judge is the ultimate gatekeeper in deciding which trials will be jury trials.

Some judges appear to make their decision based on what is at stake in the case. The more at stake, the better your chances of getting before a jury. On the other hand, if the injury is small, it's likely that the judge will either force both sides into a productive mediation, or worse, simply dismiss the case before it reaches a jury. Statistically, federal judges often dismiss discrimination cases by applying the agency's defenses in a very strict manner.

Obviously, the best cases to try in front of a jury are those cases that would enrage an average citizen. For example, a sexual harassment case in which a federal employee endured unwelcome sexual advances for at least a year and involved physical touching is something that would disgust most juries. It is likely that a jury would focus on the human and moving parts of the case, which would be to your benefit. In contrast, an administrative judge might focus on the technical elements, or in laymen's terms, the "legal loopholes" that might somehow let the agency off the hook.

However, there are some cases that are much better to be tried before an administrative judge. For example, a jury may not feel very sympathetic to lost training opportunities or a 120-day detail. A typical juror might think, "Look buddy, life's not perfect. We've all had bosses we didn't like and that doesn't mean every single time the ball doesn't bounce your way, you're entitled to a lawsuit."

Furthermore, a layperson (particularly one unfamiliar with the federal employment system) may not be able to fully appreciate the value of lost training opportunities. In this type of case, an administrative judge would be a preferable trier of fact. Not only will he or she be familiar with the realities of federal employment, but the administrative judge is more likely to look at the case from a technical standpoint. In other words, if you've suffered discrimination, then you're technically entitled to compensation and attorney fees, no matter how slight the damages might appear to the layperson.

As you can see, the decision as to the proper forum to bring your action can be complicated. Once again, this may be a good time to consult with an attorney who concentrates in representing federal employees in discrimination claims. A seasoned practitioner can provide valuable insights that can make a substantial difference in the outcome you achieve. After all, some forums are certainly better than others in particular cases.

Finally, we must point out that the administrative hearing process is far more user friendly than the federal court system. The rules for navigating through the federal court system (as well as local rules of each district court) must be followed to the letter. Even one slip up could cause a dismissal.

Therefore, if you're bringing your case in federal court, you need an attorney who practices in this area. Technically, it's possible to proceed *pro se* (without an attorney), but it's highly unlikely that you'll get the results you're entitled to. In fact, over the years, we've had clients retain us after they had attempted to bring their cases *pro se.* In one case, at the very first conference, the judge ordered the *pro se* litigant to get an attorney.

And while an attorney is almost a necessity in federal court, it's often helpful in an administrative hearing as well. And fortunately, if you are successful, the agency may be ordered to pay your attorney fees. In fact, even if you just settle your claim with the agency (which is likely considering that up to 60% of all complaints are settled at the administrative hearing level), you can often arrange to have your fees and costs paid by the agency.

Chapter 12
Requesting a Hearing

For purposes of this book, let's assume that you choose to start the decision making process by requesting a hearing before an administrative judge. To do so, you must submit a request for a hearing to the appropriate EEOC district or field office. The acceptance letter you received from the agency after filing your formal complaint should contain the address and contact information for this office.

There is no universally prescribed form for this request. You may receive a request form from the agency, or you might not. If not, then simply mail a letter similar to the one set forth on the next page. Also, you must send a copy of this request to the Director of Equal Employment Opportunity for your agency.

Although you can make this request at any time after the 180-day window has closed (we recommend sooner rather than later), your time for doing so is limited once the EEO Investigator has finished his or her report. In that case, you only have 30 days after receiving the ROI to make your request for a hearing. If you fail to make the request on time, you will lose out on your opportunity to have a hearing (unless there is some extenuating circumstance justifying your tardiness).

At that point, your only options will be to appeal the final agency determination that will be issued (to the EEOC OFO) or to take your case to federal court. Therefore, we strongly urge you to prepare your hearing request well ahead of time. In fact, we suggest that you have the request ready well before the end of the 180-day investigative period, so that you can drop it in the mail on Day 181.

And while you are at it, if the investigator misses the deadline (which is likely), you might want to consider asking for sanctions against the agency for its delay in completing the investigation. On the following page, we've provided a very simple form of hearing request. A more involved sample is provided in Appendix A to this book.

SAMPLE HEARING REQUEST

EEOC Hearings Unit

_____ District/Field Office

_____

_____

_____

Dear Sir/Madam:

I am requesting the appointment of an Equal Employment Opportunity Commission Administrative Judge pursuant to 29 C.F.R. § 1614.109(g). I hereby certify that either more than 180 days have passed from the date I filed my complaint or I have received a notice from the agency that I have thirty (30) days to elect a hearing or a final agency decision.

My name: _____

Agency
Name &
Address: _____

_____

_____

_____

Agency
Number: _____

In accordance with section 1614.108(g), I have sent a copy of this request for a hearing to the following person at the agency:

Name: _____

Address: _____

_____

_____

_____

Sincerely,

[Your Name]

Chapter 13

The Acknowledgment Order

Once you file your request for a hearing, the agency has 15 days to send a copy of the complaint to the appropriate EEOC field or district office. The EEOC will then appoint an administrative judge to preside over your hearing. The AJ assumes full responsibility for the deciding the issues set forth in the complaint at this point.

The AJ assigned to your case will issue an Acknowledgment Order, which is the formal document describing the litigation schedule for your case.

The Acknowledgment Order is perhaps the most important document in the early stages of your case. In fact, if the schedule set forth in this document isn't followed to the letter, the AJ may dismiss your case. The Acknowledgment Order can be very intimidating for non-lawyers. For this reason, our office gets many calls from federal employees who originally file discrimination cases on their own, but later realize that they don't have a clue how to respond to the Acknowledgment Order.

One of the most intimidating aspects of the Acknowledgment Order is the adverse consequences for failing to comply with it in all respects. For example, we once had a client come to us after originally hiring a "lawyer" who wasn't actually licensed to practice law (we believe he's now in jail). In any event, the previous "attorney" had missed an important deadline with regard to a pre-hearing statement as described in the Acknowledgment Order. As a result, the AJ dismissed the case in its entirety. Our client had to appeal the dismissal before the case could even continue.

Therefore, it should go without saying, that you should take the Acknowledgment Order very seriously. Read through it several times, paying particular attention to the deadlines set forth in the document. And, by all means, make sure that you comply with *all* of its instructions.

The Acknowledgment Order will generally set forth:

- the length of discovery

- the types of discovery allowed

- any limitations on discovery (i.e., how many interrogatories, how many requests for admission, etc.)

- how long a party has to respond to discovery

- what to do if the other side does not respond to discovery (i.e., file a Motion to Compel)

- set forth procedures and time frames

The Acknowledgment Order may also contain a provision requiring submission of witness lists by a certain date, and may require submission of a Prehearing Statement (and describe in detail what must be contained in that document). The AO is a critical document and must be treated accordingly.

If you need an extension of time, you should call the opposing party representative (usually an Office of the General Counsel attorney-advisor) and try to get them to agree. If you cannot get an extension, or if the other side does not oppose it, you still need to inform (or request an extension from) the administrative judge. We have had instances where both sides agree to an extension or other modification of the time frames, and the AJ refused, so be prepared to stick to the original schedule.

Chapter 14

Pre-Hearing Discovery

Up until this point, you will have played a fairly passive role in the fact-finding process. You had no power to direct the EEO Counselor or the EEO Investigator to speak with certain witnesses. Sure, you could make suggestions and provide names and contact information, but the counselor and investigator were free to ignore your recommendations. And even if they made contact with the right people, there was no guarantee that they would ask the right questions.

Well, all of that changes when you reach the discovery phase. For the first time, you are in the driver's seat. You (and your attorney, if you have one) get to determine who will be interviewed and what they will be asked. In short, it's at this point when *you* finally start to make your case.

As you probably know, the purpose of discovery is to supplement the factual record so that everyone's cards are out on the table, so to speak. And while it may be disconcerting to think that this work was not done by the EEOC Investigator during the six months he or she had to complete the task, the ability to conduct discovery is a great benefit to you.

This is true even in those rare cases where the investigator *appears* to have conducted a thorough investigation of your claims. As we all know, appearances can be deceiving. An ROI can appear to be complete and yet, be anything but. Remember, what's not in the ROI is as important as what is in it.

For example, let's suppose you allege in your complaint that you were the victim of gender discrimination. In particular, you allege that you were passed over for a promotion, which went instead to someone of the opposite gender.

During the investigation, the investigator spoke with your boss, who gave several plausible sounding explanations for the promotion decision. Furthermore, the investigator obtained copies of your last performance review and the most recent performance review of the person who was promoted in your stead. During this review period, that person did, in fact, receive a higher appraisal. On its face, it appears that your boss' decision was legitimate and wasn't the result of any gender bias.

However, there may be (and usually are) other facts not contained in the factual record that could lead to a different conclusion. For example, let's suppose you scored significantly higher than your counterpart during four of the last five review periods and that your *only* inferior performance review was the most recent one. Furthermore, let's suppose your department has, in the past, given priority based on seniority. Yet, for some reason, this rule was not applied in your case. The seemingly "complete" factual record may make no mention of these facts.

Fortunately, discovery allows you to gather information to prove your case. Discovery allows you to request the production of all performance reviews for your counterpart and yourself over, say, the last three years. Likewise, you may request the production of all written policies regarding the seniority preference. If the rule was unwritten, then you may request to depose (i.e., question) any agency employee with knowledge of this informal rule.

In fact, you may request any and all information from the agency, provided that you can demonstrate that your request is reasonable and likely to result in the development of relevant evidence in the case. This is your right under the law and you shouldn't be shy in asserting it. So long as you can demonstrate that your request for supplemental information is reasonable and relevant, the AJ should allow it.

Typical Time Frames for Discovery

Now, usually the Acknowledgment Order will provide you with only 20 or 30 days to initiate discovery. This simply means you must get discovery *started* within this time frame. Therefore, it is imperative that you not let these twenty days expire without making at least one discovery demand on the agency. Your request should be sent directly to the agency representative, and not the AJ (although some AJs will want to receive notice that your discovery request has been served).

Different Types of Discovery You Can Request

In making your request, you can ask the agency to respond to any and all of the following:

1)   Interrogatories
2)   Depositions
3)   Stipulations

4)   Requests for Admissions

5)   Requests for the Production of Documents

Discovery is where you can prove your case, or where the agency can prove that you have no case. Or it can be where you prove that there is a dispute that needs to be resolved at a hearing. Discovery is the mechanism by which facts are found, theories are proven, lies are uncovered and the truth can be shown. Discovery is not just for attorneys, although it can be complicated. One of the main points of this book is to help you get through the discovery phase of your case, hopefully knowing more afterwards than when you entered into it. We don't consider this legal advice, and you should consult with an experienced attorney when using or adapting any form we provide.

In the following chapters, we will discuss each of these discovery techniques in detail.

Chapter 15

Interrogatories

Interrogatories (the modern form of "interrogation") are written questions that require a written response from the other party. The purpose of interrogatories is to provide you with general information about the agency's defense to the case that the investigator failed to get. You can then use these interrogatory responses to probe further into the true reasons agency officials acted as they did. You can force the agency to create or gather information, rather than just providing information that already exists in a particular form.

For example, let's suppose you've brought a disparate impact claim under Title VII and you'd like to obtain demographic information from your agency's head of personnel. If you depose this person, it's unlikely that they will know off-hand, say, the percentage of female Asian Americans who have been promoted to the GS-14 level in the last five years. In this case, an interrogatory is your best chance of getting this information, because it allows the head of personnel to comb his or her files in response to your question.

While interrogatories are certainly a useful tool in the discovery arsenal, please note that they can't be overused. You can usually only send out interrogatories all at one time (depending on the AJ), and that one set of interrogatories can have no more than thirty (30) questions. And you can't get around the 30 question limit by asking in questions in multiple subparts. Each part or subpart of question counts towards your maximum of 30. The only exception to this limit is if you get specific authorization from the AJ, or an agreement from the agency, to send out additional interrogatories.

In Appendix B, you'll find a sample set of interrogatories that we prepared for a client in his case against the Department of Veteran Affairs. This was a case involving gender discrimination. We discovered in the ROI that the male who ultimately received the promotion wasn't willing to transfer to another location – a requirement of the position. In our interrogatories, we honed in on this discrepancy and asked the selecting official to advise us if it knew about the selectee's inability to meet the requirements of the job before choosing him for the position.

We used these interrogatories to help determine our strategy during the selecting official's deposition. If the selecting official answered that he knew about the selectee's inability to meet the transfer requirement, we would ask why that didn't matter. On the other hand, if the selecting official was unaware of this situation, we would be ready with a completely different set of questions. For instance, we would ask, "How is it that you didn't know? Wasn't it right on his application in black and white? What else didn't you see? How much time did you spend reading these applications?" And so on. Either way, we would be able to call into question the propriety of this decision.

You'll also notice we asked questions about the selectee's corporate audit experience, as this was a key component of the position and our client advised us that she had performed many more audits than the selectee. We're happy to report that not long after we served these interrogatories and pressed the agency for answers, the case settled and our client received the promotion.

A major reason why we wrote this book was to give you samples that you could use in your own discrimination case. Please feel free to use the interrogatories contained in Appendix B, and available for download at our website, as a template. Of course, keep in mind, that these interrogatories were narrowly tailored to the situation presented. Therefore, you will need to modify them to fit the specifics of your case.

Chapter 16

Depositions

A deposition is an in-person question and answer session in which the witness (the deponent) is questioned by you or your attorney. In a deposition, the deponent provides testimony under oath. Also, a written transcript of the deposition is produced by a third-party, such as a court reporter. This written transcript becomes part of the factual record.

When to Depose

Often, a deposition is the quickest and easiest way to gather testimony from a witness. For example, if you've brought a hostile work environment claim, another co-worker may be able to corroborate your claims of harassment. If this person is still employed by the agency and lives within a reasonable distance of you, it's a simple matter to depose this person and get his or her comments on the record. Also, since this person need only testify as to what they saw and heard on a particular date (or dates), there isn't a need to submit written interrogatories, which often call for much more detailed and researched responses.

Furthermore, depositions provide an important advantage not available through interrogatories – the opportunity to seek immediate clarification and elaboration. The responses to your interrogatories are set in stone. If they are unclear or incomplete, then you are most likely stuck with them, unless you file a motion to compel a more detailed and thorough response (this is explained in more detail in a later chapter). However, even then, you will be required to expend additional time and effort, as you must serve this motion on the other party, allow them to time to respond, and then have a hearing before the AJ to determine if you are indeed entitled to more elaboration on their response.

How to Corner a Witness in a Deposition

Fortunately, none of these steps are necessary in a deposition. If you don't like the response you get to a particular question, you can simply follow it up with another question. For example, let's suppose you're deposing a co-worker, who was an eyewitness to one of the many instances of sexual harassment you experienced on the job. While your co-worker is sympathetic to your case, she is reluctant to testify on your behalf for fear of retaliation. Nevertheless, as a federal employee, she has been compelled by the AJ to appear for your deposition.

During the deposition, you establish that the two of you were having lunch in the lunchroom one day when Mr. Smith entered. You further establish that Mr. Smith walked over to you and put his hands on your shoulders and began playing with your hair. At this point, you may ask, "Is it true that Mr. Smith then said to me, 'You know you want me, babe?'" Surprisingly, the witness answers, "No!"

If this was the response to a written interrogatory, you'd be stuck. However, in a deposition, you can simply say, "OK, what is your recollection of what he said?" In this case, the deponent says, "Well, what he actually said was, 'You know you've been wanting me for a long time now, babe.'"

Depositions also give you a chance to clarify otherwise incomplete answers. For example, let's suppose you're deposing your former boss, whom you believe has fired you for a discriminatory reason. During the deposition, you ask her why she fired you. She replies, "Because your performance was poor."

By itself, this answer sounds good for the agency, but it is far from being a complete answer. How is your boss defining "poor performance"? How does this determination of poor performance jibe with the "outstanding performance" ratings that you received on your last three reviews? During a deposition, you get the opportunity to seek immediate answers to these questions.

Whom to Depose

It is always to your advantage to depose the agency decision makers – the persons who made the decision to take the adverse action against you. You want to get each decision maker's story and the step-by-step actions each took in the process of making their decisions.

And don't be afraid to ask questions at the deposition to which the agency witness will give an answer not favorable to your case. In fact, you should expect that. The point is to find out this information well *before* the hearing. Knowing this information will help you to determine which questions to ask (and equally important, which questions *not* to ask) at your hearing.

Obtaining a Deposition Transcript

Finally, before taking any depositions, you'll have to arrange for a court reporting company to appear at the deposition and transcribe the testimony into written form. Following the deposition, the court reporter will send you a copy of each witness transcript. The reporting company generally charges anywhere from $3 to $5 a page.

Yet, this fee is well worth it. A deposition transcript is useful for two purposes. First, it helps you to form your opposition if the agency files a Motion for Summary Judgment (this will be explained in detail in a later chapter). Second, it helps to keep witnesses honest at the hearing. If a witness' story deviates from the one given during the deposition, you will be able to impeach that witness with his deposition. We will discuss this concept more fully in a later chapter.

Chapter 17

Stipulations

Stipulations are points of facts upon which the parties readily agree. For example, both you and the agency should be able to agree upon the dates of your employment and your position within the agency. Furthermore, you should be able to agree on other facts that are easily verifiable. The purpose of a stipulation is to pave the way for both sides to make their case without wasting time introducing documents and evidence to prove points that are not in dispute.

For instance, without the ability to make stipulations, you might have to call the head of personnel to testify at your hearing to prove that you were indeed employed by the agency. Likewise, you might have to call every co-worker in your department to prove, say, that you are the person with the most seniority. This would obviously be a great waste of everyone's time. Therefore, if both parties can stipulate to some of the basic underlying facts, the AJ can turn his or her attention to ruling on the relatively few issues that are still in dispute. For this reason, AJs greatly encourage the parties to stipulate whenever issues of fact are not in dispute.

That being said, you can't expect too much from stipulations. For example, in a racial discrimination case, you aren't going to get the agency to stipulate that you've been the victim of racial discrimination; at least, not likely. However, it may be possible to get the agency to stipulate to the fact that, on a particular occasion, your boss used a particular racial slur. While this may not completely prove your claim of racial discrimination, it will prevent you from calling the 25 witnesses to this statement at your hearing.

On the next page, we've provided a sample stipulation used in a case against the U.S. Postal Service. In this case, our client, who was sensitive to extreme cold temperature, filed a complaint in an effort to get the Postal Service to accommodate her condition and assign her work in a warmer area. Together, our client and the Postal Service stipulated to certain testimony so that we could avoid calling these witnesses at the hearing.

JOINT STIPULATIONS AND AGREEMENTS OF THE PARTIES

The Complainant, by and through her attorney, Snider Law Offices, Michael J. Snider, Esq., and the Agency, by and through its Counsel, Attorney Idont Getalong Withyou, hereby submit these Joint Stipulations and Agreements of the Parties in this case, and state:

Stipulations

In an attempt to facilitate the timely and efficient processing of the Complaint at issue, the Parties agree to Stipulate as follows:

The Parties Stipulate that, if called, [Witness #1] would testify to his expertise in HVAC (CV Attached hereto).

The Parties Stipulate that, if called, [Witness #1] would testify that the discharge temperature at the vents in the IMF near the Complainant's work station would be within five (5) degrees of the temperature indicated on the Cabinet Point Log as "DISC TEMP."

The Parties Stipulate that, if called, [Witness #1] would testify that the effect of closing the louvers on the discharge vents at the IMF would be to dissipate the air coming out of the vent, but not to stop the air entirely.

The Parties Stipulate that, if called, [Witness #2] would testify that she knows the Complainant and has witnessed the Complainant on her smoke breaks.

The Parties Stipulate that, if called, [Witness #2] would testify that she and Complainant smoked outside during break times around three times per night, that while [Witness #2] would stand outside, Complainant would stand just outside the door, but right near the door so that the warmer inside air would blow out onto her.

The Parties Stipulate that, if called, [Witness #2] would testify that she understood that Complainant did this in order to stay warm because the cold negatively affected her.

The Parties Stipulate that, if called, [Witness #2] would testify that the smoke breaks were 3 minutes each, at the most.

The Parties Stipulate that, if called, [Witness #2] would testify that, in her opinion, taking smoke breaks in the cold does not make Ms. Client less believable that the cold bothers her back, because (at least when [Witness #2] worked in the IMF on the floor in 1999) it was cold.

Agreements

The Parties agree that, in lieu of calling [Witness #3] or [Witness #4] as witnesses, their Deposition transcripts may be entered into the record as evidence, without objection.

The Agency has no opposition to the adding of one (1) live witness (either _____, _____, or _____) to testify as proffered in Complainant's Pre-Hearing Statement, in addition to Complainant and Dr. _____.

Respectfully Submitted,

_____   _____
Idont Getalong Withyou, Esq.   Michael J. Snider, Esq.
Agency Representative   Complainant's Representative

Chapter 18

Requests for Admissions

Requests for admissions are very similar to stipulations, except that they are admissions by one party while stipulations require an agreement of both parties. Yet, the principle involved is the same – to save the time and effort of calling multiple witnesses whose testimony is not in dispute.

The use of admissions is quite common in authenticating documents. For example, if your performance reviews are at issue in the case, you don't want to be forced to hire a handwriting expert to prove that your boss signed on the bottom line of the evaluation, unless, of course, your boss is denying doing so. Otherwise, a simple request for your boss to admit that he signed the performance review will do the trick.

And while requests for admissions are encouraged in most cases, parties have been known to overdo them. As a result, unless you receive specific authorization from the AJ to do otherwise, you can only submit requests for up to thirty (30) admissions. As in the case of interrogatories, admissions requested in subparts count towards the total. However, for this purpose, admissions relating to the authenticity of documents are not usually counted towards the limit of 30.

In Appendix C, we have provided a sample of a request for admissions. In looking through this sample, pay particular attention to how much witness testimony is avoided by having the respondent admit to certain facts beforehand.

Of course, please note that, as the name implies, a request for admissions is just that; a *request*. The other party can, and very often will, refuse to admit various points along the way. As a result, these points become the main focus at the hearing, as each side introduces its own witnesses in an attempt to prove that a certain event occurred (or did not occur).

Chapter 19

Requests for Production of Documents

In order to make your case, you will often need documentary evidence, such as performance reviews, medical records, etc. In some cases, these documents will be in your files. For example, you may have kept copies of all of your performance reviews. By the way, if you haven't, we suggest that you do from now on. However, in some cases, you won't have copies (or even access) to these documents.

For example, you almost certainly won't have access to the personnel file of someone who has been promoted (perhaps, wrongly) in front of you. In this case, to prove that you were actually more qualified for the position, you will need access to their personnel file. In other cases, you may need copies of other documents, such as the minutes of managers' meetings, written policies of the agency, etc.

In making your request for the production of documents, you should be as specific as possible. You don't need to know the exact title of the document or its form number, but you should identify the document with enough specificity so that there can be no disputes as to the document you are requesting. Also, your request shouldn't be overbroad in that you ask for "All documents relating to the employment of Jane Doe."

In fact, to ease the burden of the other party, you are only allowed to ask for up to thirty (30) different documents (or sets of documents). Once again, the same rule regarding subparts applies to document requests. However, in counting requests, documents of a particular type may be grouped together as just one document for purposes of the 30 document limit. For example, the request for all performance reviews of Jane Doe from January 1, 2000 to December 31, 2004 may be treated as a single document request.

At the end of this chapter, we've provided a sample request for the production of documents to give you an idea of how such a request may be made in practice.

Responding to the Agency's Request for Production

Just like you have the right to serve discovery, so does the agency. You have to keep track of every shred of paper that you produce, and make sure that you are very careful to produce every document that you might want to use at the hearing (with a few exceptions which we will cover later). If the agency asks for something, and you fail to object to its production, you have to produce it or risk being sanctioned. Some sanctions could include an adverse inference on the subject matter, having testimony on the matter excluded or even an adverse decision by the AJ on that issue.

So there is no dispute over what you produced, you should 1) create a comprehensive index of the documents you produce and 2) make an entire set of everything you produce to the agency and set it aside "just in case." You should consider buying or borrowing a "Bates Stamp," which numbers pages sequentially, or using a photocopy machine which will do the same thing – insert a number on each page. That way, if the agency ever claims you didn't provide them with a document (usually this occurs at the hearing when you move to introduce a really juicy document and they scream bloody murder), you can point out to the AJ that you not only did produce it, but you brought an index of what you produced **and** a complete copy of all documents delivered to the agency.

EQUAL EMPLOYMENT OPPORTUNITY COMMISSION
BALTIMORE FIELD OFFICE
10 South Howard Street
Baltimore, MD 21201

Jane Doe,)	
)	
COMPLAINANT,)	EEOC NO. XXX-XXXX-XXXXXX
)	
vs.)	
)	AGENCY CASE NO.: XXXXX
Department of Defense,)	
Defense Contact Audit Agency)	
)	
AGENCY.)	
)	

COMPLAINANT'S REQUEST FOR PRODUCTION OF DOCUMENTS

The Complainant, through her attorney, Morris E. Fischer, Esq. of Snider and Fischer LLC, requests that the Agency respond to the following request for production of documents. You are required to respond to this request no later than thirty (30) calendar days after receipt of this Request for the Production of Documents. Your response(s) and the documents are to be sent to the undersigned at 104 Church Lane Suite 201, Baltimore, Maryland 21208.

1. Please provide a complete copy of the Complainant's file and any other files maintained by the Agency regarding or referencing the Complainant. Said files are to be in its non-purged form and content. In the event any documents of any kind or nature whatsoever have been removed from said file, name the person in whose care, custody or possession such documents are at, and the reason for their removal.

2. Please provide a complete copy of the Selectee's file and any other files maintained by the Agency regarding or referencing the selectee. Said files are to be in its non-purged form and content. In the event any documents of any kind or nature whatsoever have been removed from said file, name the person in whose care, custody or possession such documents are at, and the reason for their removal.

3. Please provide copies of any documents referred to or relied upon in your answers to interrogatories.

4. All organizational charts which include all employees in the direct supervision of _____ and _____ for the previous five years.

5.   All documents you intend to enter into evidence at a dispositive hearing or trial in this case.

6.   Provide copies of any and all correspondence between Agency officials, supervisors, managers or other management officials including Team Leaders, persons from the Human Relations or Personnel Department of the Agency pertaining to any matter or issue raised in this case.

7.   Provide a copy of any information contained in the promotion package in this case, including rating sheets, interview questions, ranking, etc.

8.   Provide all notes written by and records kept by all individuals with input into the subject position regarding this selection process.

9.   Provide all emails, memos or any other communications about recommendations for this promotion.

10. Copy of the SF-171 or resume and any other documents submitted by the Selectee in application for the subject position.

11. Copy of the SF-171 or resume and any other documents submitted by Complainant in application for the subject position.

12. Copies of individual ratings of applicants completed by the HR staff and/or the CMP on all applicants for the above position.

13. Copy of the Mobility Agreement signed by the Selectee referenced in the Remarks on the promotion SF-50 dated November 3, 2002 following his selection for the subject position.

Respectfully Submitted,

Date:_____   _____

                                                Morris E. Fischer , Esq.
                                                Attorney for Complainant

Chapter 20

Responding to Agency Discovery

As you have probably guessed, discovery is a two-way street. Just as you have the right to seek discovery from the agency, the agency has the right to seek discovery from you. So be prepared to get a thick package from the agency entitled something really intimidating like "Agency's Combined First Set of Interrogatories, Requests for Admission, Requests for Production and Notice of Deposition." The package will be intentionally hefty, if for no other reason than to intimidate you into thinking "What have I gotten myself into?"

Well, **don't be intimidated**. None of the agency's requests of you will be any different from the requests you can ask of it. That's the reason we spent so much time on them in the preceding chapters – to get you familiar with them so that they won't look so intimidating.

However, to save yourself some time in answering these requests, we suggest you ask the agency to email you a copy of the documents. That way, you can type your answers right into the document instead of retyping it.

When Must You Respond?

It is very important to answer the agency's discovery request in a timely manner. Remember, your failure to do so could result in the AJ dismissing your case. So what is "timely?" It depends on the AJ's Acknowledgment Order. In some cases, you will have 30 days to respond. In other cases, you will have 20 days to respond.

If you're unable to respond within this time period, you can request a 15-day extension from the agency. Make sure that if the agency grants your extension, you get it in writing.

Also be sure (*very* sure) that none of your answers are different from what you said in your statements to the counselor or the investigator. If so, the agency will try to use your previous responses against you to show that you aren't being consistent (i.e., truthful).

If the agency misses its deadline for submitting its discovery request to you (and this happens more often than you would think), you still have to file objections in a timely manner, stating that you object to responding because they were untimely. Drag out a calendar in any case and count off the days – you never know. If they are late, and they haven't asked you or the AJ for an extension, you could get lucky and not have to respond at all. Of course, if your discovery is untimely as well, you may be better off with an agreement that both sides will answer, rather than both of you getting to summary judgment or a hearing without any idea as to what the other side has in store.

Chapter 21

Your Deposition

In almost all cases, you will be deposed. It would be utterly foolish of the agency not to depose you. After all, they usually use one, and sometimes two, attorneys on every single case. They are spending so much money on these cases (when they could save money by settling most of them) that throwing good money after bad is not a problem for them. Therefore, unless the agency lawyer is totally asleep at the wheel (and fortunately, we've had cases like that), expect to be deposed. This means you will be answering the agency attorney's questions, under oath, with a court reporter and possibly the RMO in the room to boot.

Sadly, this is precisely the point in the proceedings where many employees lose their entire case. This happens because they often don't understand the purpose of a deposition. As a result, they end up saying either the wrong things or not saying the right things.

To help you avoid this pitfall, we'll uncover some of the major traps that agency attorneys attempt to set for unwary complainants. We'll also discuss some of the most common mistakes we've seen made by complainants in their depositions.

Tell the Truth

However, before getting into that discussion, let us take just a moment to state the obvious – you must answer *all* questions truthfully in your deposition. You will be testifying under penalty of perjury, and while perjury convictions are somewhat rare in these types of cases, they do happen. A perjury conviction often entails jail time, a hefty fine and will wreak havoc on your future employment prospects; so don't risk it.

And even if you're never charged with a crime, you ruin any chance of winning your case if you give the AJ reason to suspect that you're being less than truthful. As your credibility is your most important asset, you want to guard it zealously, even against inadvertent misrepresentations.

For this reason, when testifying in your deposition, you should attempt to leave your answer open-ended, when the situation warrants. For example, if you're asked to list *every* event relating to the discriminatory action, make sure to preference your answer with something like: "I will try to list all events, but my memory is a little hazy and I might not remember everything right now. I reserve the right to add to my answer in the future." If you later remember additional events after the deposition (and you often will), you don't want to put yourself in a position where you seem to be "inventing" additional incidents at the hearing.

Prepare for the Deposition

One way to avoid inadvertent misstatements of fact is to prepare carefully for the deposition. Don't walk in cold. Prepare a chronological list of what happened, who did it, who witnessed it, what proof you have that it occurred. For instance, did you go to the doctor the next day? Did you mention it to your spouse or a co-worker or a friend right after it happened? Did you keep a daily diary? And make sure that you bring supporting documentation with you to the deposition (if you haven't already given it to the investigator, or to the agency in your responses to their discovery requests).

Take Your Time

We're not going to lie to you, depositions are stressful. It's downright nerve racking to be on the "hot seat," knowing that the agency attorney is just waiting for you to say one wrong thing so that he or she can pounce on you.

For this reason, many people attempt to rush their way through the deposition in an attempt to "get it over with." This is a recipe for disaster. Therefore, we strongly recommend that you take your time in both listening to the questions and giving your answers.

Don't Answer a Question You Don't Fully Understand

Obviously, at a minimum, you should make sure that you fully understand the question you're attempting to answer. And remember, this may be different than the question you *think* has been answered. Therefore, before blurting out an answer, make 100% sure that you understand the question.

And if you are the *slightest* bit unsure, then ask the agency attorney to repeat the question. If it's still unclear, ask him or her to rephrase the question. And even then, confirm that you truly understand the question.

"Let's just make sure that I understand you correctly here. What you're asking is..."

This is particularly true when dealing with double negatives. It can be extremely confusing when two or more negatives get mixed into a question. In fact, it can get downright impossible to answer. For instance, you could be asked, "Is it not true that you were not promoted not because of your race but rather because of poor work performance?" In this case, does a "yes" answer mean that you were passed over because of your race or that you were not selected for poor work performance? Who knows?

Therefore, if you're asked a question like this (and you probably will be), don't even attempt to answer it. Ask the agency attorney to clarify the question so that it's possible for you (and everyone else) to know what you're answering "yes" or "no" to.

Now, please understand that we're not suggesting that you adapt this technique as a method to drag out the deposition and wear down your opponent. We're simply suggesting that you don't inadvertently give an answer that sinks your case because you didn't fully understand the question.

Don't Answer the Question Until It's Been Fully Asked

You must be careful to allow the agency attorney to ask the full question before attempting to answer. Even if you think you know where the question is headed, let the attorney finish the question. The agency isn't paying you to represent its interests, so don't do the agency attorney's job for her.

This is most likely to happen when there is a slight weakness in your case. For instance, let's suppose that you've filed an age discrimination case because you were not selected for a promotion that you deserved. Instead, the promotion went to a much younger person with significantly less experience. You know that one of the weaknesses of your case is that you had a less than glowing review in the 2nd quarter of 2001.

In preparing for your deposition, you anticipate being questioned about this review and are prepared to explain that your performance level dropped very briefly as your mother was in the last stages of Alzheimer's at the time and you were driving back and forth to her home 200 miles away every weekend during this period. Furthermore, you're prepared to explain how your performance before and after this period has been exemplary.

Therefore, as soon as the agency attorney gets to the issue of your work record, you mentally prepare yourself to explain your one bad review. The agency attorney starts her question, "So you think you were more qualified than Mr. So and So. Well, if that's the case, how do you expla--." And before she can finish, you launch into your explanation.

Yet, in your haste to speed up the deposition, you may have just given the agency more ammunition in its battle against you. Incredibly, the agency attorney may have completely glossed over your bad review. Instead, she was going to ask your boss' allegations that you have a bad attitude, an allegation that has been refuted by every witness interviewed by the investigator. Yet, because you didn't wait to hear the full question, you've just given the agency another basis upon which to possibly justify your boss's promotion decision.

Answer Only the Question Asked of You

A corollary to jumping the gun and not waiting for the agency attorney to finish his or her question is to answer more than just the question asked of you. This often happens when you think you know the agency attorney's next logical question, so why waste the time in waiting for him to ask it? Well, as we demonstrated above, you don't know the agency attorney's next question. By answering a question that hasn't yet been asked, you're doing that person's job for them.

Also, we've seen many times when anxiety causes the witness to just start blurting out things as a form of nervous chatter. These types of comments can have disastrous consequences for your case.

For example, using the previous example, you're being deposed as part of your age discrimination complaint. The agency attorney asks you if you really think that you were more qualified than the person selected and you say, "Absolutely! I was much more qualified. However, I have to admit, So and So is doing a great job in the position." That wasn't the question!

The question was simply were you more qualified for the promotion. By volunteering your "opinion" about the selectee's superb job performance, you've weakened your own case that you should have received the promotion. Of course, this is an extreme example but you'd be surprised at how often we've seen witnesses make extraneous remarks that were devastating to their cases.

Top Five Damaging Statements You Can Make

In fact, we've prepared a list of the five of the most damaging statements employees make at their depositions:

Damaging Statement #1: "He was a Union Guy"

We know of at least one case in which the deposition went as follows:

Agency Attorney: *"So, why do you think the promotion to the Grade 13 went to the selectee, Mr. So and So?"*

Complainant: *"Well, I'll tell ya. He came down from New York and had all these fancy connections and he was well connected to the union. He was a union guy. Boy, they were scared of him!"*

At that very moment, this person lost her case. Remember, if you were passed over for the position, harassed, reassigned, etc. for any reason *other* than discrimination, you *don't have* a case that can be resolved in the EEO forum. To prevail at the hearing, you must convince the AJ that you were the victim of discrimination in violation of Title VII, the ADEA, the Rehab Act/ADA or the EPA. At the very least, if you can't prove outright discrimination, you must convince the AJ that there was no other plausible explanation for the decision.

Therefore, if you assert in your deposition that Mr. So and So got the position because he was a <u>union</u> guy and they were scared of him (and <u>not</u> because of your race, gender, nationality, disability, etc.), you are saying that you *don't have an EEO case.* A much better answer would have been: "I believe race was a factor here because there has never been a minority person selected for that position since Mr. Racist took over as the selecting official."

Damaging Statement #2: "I Was Just as Qualified as the Person Who Got Promoted"

You can't base your discrimination claim on the fact that you were *just as qualified as* the other person. The legal standard for proving discrimination is that you were **more** qualified. In fact, you had to be *substantially* more qualified.

Therefore, at your deposition, you must be prepared to not only state that you were substantially more qualified, but to explain why, and to do so in great detail. If you can't do so, you can expect the agency lawyer to argue to the AJ that your case should be dismissed. And you can expect this argument to be persuasive to the AJ. After all, if you don't even believe that you were substantially more qualified than the selectee, why would the AJ?

Damaging Statement #3: "Silly, Stupid Stuff"

You shouldn't use any language that minimizes the harm you've suffered as a result of the unlawful discrimination. For instance, in a hostile work environment case, the agency attorney may say, "Tell me all the things that made your environment hostile." Your answer should not be something like, "They took my chair away several times. They were on my computer downloading pornography. They did stuff to me that was annoying. I mean, it was a lot of really silly, stupid stuff."

To prevail on a hostile work environment claim, you have to show that the actions taken were *not only* severe or pervasive, but that you felt either physically threatened or humiliated. On the other hand, if you considered the stuff they did just "silly and stupid," your annoyance doesn't rise to the level of an actionable claim under the EEO process. In short, by reducing your co-workers' actions to the level of a high school class under the guidance of a substitute teacher, you've seriously damaged your case.

In that situation, here's a much better answer to the question:

"The actions taken against me on a daily basis were serious and humiliating. My co-workers would invade my workspace right in front of me. They would remove my chair when I was about to sit down on almost every occasion they could. There were many times when I fell right on my buttocks in front of the whole office, including my supervisor. While I would be sitting in pain, my co-workers would be high-fiving each other; saying that they had 'given that cripple another opportunity to get off her behind and climb the government ladder.' When I wasn't looking, my co-workers would then download pornography on my computer and ridicule me several times per week about my screensavers. They would make comments like... "

This response is superior because it's fact driven, verifiable and demonstrates how the harassment was severe, pervasive and caused you to be physically threatened and humiliated.

Damaging Statement #4: I'm Tough, So It Didn't Bother Me

This is a distant cousin to the "silly, stupid stuff" answer. It occurs when the complainant testifies that he or she is tough, and therefore, the obnoxious behavior didn't bother them. While this stance may be heroic, it can also fatal to your case. Remember, in a hostile work environment claim, you must have been subjectively threatened or humiliated. If you were too tough to be affected by the hostile environment, then the AJ is likely to say "tough luck" with regards to your case.

Now, please understand that there's an important distinction between the hostile environment *not bothering* you and you being tough enough to do your job *even though* it bothered you very much. The latter situation is OK, even admirable.

Also, being a tough guy/gal can have a negative impact on your damages award, assuming you receive one at all. Unless you can describe the great emotional effect the hostile work environment had on you and the physical symptoms you sustained as a result (e.g., depression, anxiety, weight gain, etc.), you shouldn't expect to receive a lot in compensatory damages for pain and suffering.

On the other hand, if you worried about your job and couldn't sleep at night because you knew you had to go to work the next day and face a hostile environment, that's a different story. It's a terrible situation. And if this terrible situation made you cry in front of your spouse, your children or your minister, don't be so "tough" that you don't say so. That's the kind of testimony that translates into a high compensatory damage award.

WIFE BUDA

To help our clients remember the symptoms that are most common in these situations, we use a memory pneumonic – *WIFE BUDA.*

W- Weight gain or loss
I – Insomnia
F- Inability to Focus
E- Loss of Energy

B- Blood pressure changes
U- Unwillingness to do anything
D- Depression
A- Anxiety

Damaging Statement #5: The Compensatory Damage Exaggerator

On the flip side of the coin, one of the worst things you can do is to exaggerate your injuries at either the deposition or the hearing. You don't want to appear to be someone who is milking the situation for all it's worth. Therefore, if you're claiming compensatory damages for a physical injury, make sure you supply a copy of your medical records to the agency and the AJ to back up your claim (you can also use layperson testimony to support a comp damages claim, like a spouse or parent).

And, of course, you should only testify as to those mental and physical symptoms that are supported by (or at least, not in conflict with) this medical documentation. For example, don't testify at your deposition that you had trouble sleeping and great insomnia just because you think you can rack up big bucks for pain and suffering. This is particularly good advice if your doctor's notes say something like "patient reports no trouble sleeping and does not require a prescribed sleep aid."

As we've said before, honesty is the best policy. It's not only the right thing to do, but it's the easiest. Remember, it's a piece of cake to keep your facts straight when you're telling the truth.

Agency Attorney Traps

Now, if it wasn't enough that you have to carefully watch what you say on your own, you also have to watch out for a few stumbling blocks that the agency attorney may throw in your path. Some agency attorneys will attempt to trick you into answering incorrectly by asking the question in a confusing or deceptive manner.

Of course, if you're represented by counsel at your deposition, he or she will know how to combat these tactics and raise objections on your behalf. However, if you attend the deposition without representation, then you will have to look out for yourself. Here are some types of questions to be wary of:

Compound Questions

Some agency attorneys use compound questions as a way to confuse you and twist your answers so that you don't look credible at the hearing. For example, the agency attorney may ask you, "Is it true that you hate your boss and that you think he has been sexually harassing you for the last six months?" Obviously, this is really two separate questions, the first of which is irrelevant.

But how do you answer a question like this? If you say "yes," then you are admitting to having a personal animus against your boss (which may be affecting your accurate recall of the events described in your complaint). On the other hand, if you say "no," then you are admitting that you have no case against the agency; at least for a Title VII violation.

As you probably guessed, the only correct way to answer this question is to *not* answer it. Simply explain to the agency attorney that you are being asked two separate questions and ask the agency attorney to restate them one at a time, so that you may give each question a proper answer. If the agency attorney acts dumb in this matter (and sadly, some won't be acting), then take the liberty to separate out the questions yourself.

"To answer your first question, no, I don't hate Mr. So and So. As for your second question, yes, I've been the victim of sexual harassment at the hands of Mr. So and So."

Assuming Questions

Sometimes, you will be asked a question that contains an assumption that hasn't been proven. However, by answering the question, you run the risk of indirectly affirming the assumption. As you can imagine, in most cases, the assumption is damaging to your case or your credibility as a witness.

For instance, an agency attorney may ask you, "As someone who thinks all white people are racists, is it possible that you misinterpreted your boss' comments about the Martin Luther King holiday?" In this case, even if you answer that you didn't misinterpret your boss' comments, you are still implicitly affirming the assumption that you think all white people are racists.

Therefore, once again, the best answer to this type of question is no answer. If confronted with such a question, ask the agency attorney to rephrase the question; this time, without the unwarranted assumption that you think all white people are racists.

Summary Question

Another trick used by agency attorneys is to try to get you to summarize your entire deposition in one sentence. The purpose here is to leave out important elements of your case so that it looks like you really don't have a case at all.

For example, an agency attorney may ask you, "So, in summary, what are you really saying is that you're Asian, your boss is African American and you were not promoted, so it must be racism, right?" The agency attorney is hoping that you will say something like, "Yes, that's about it," so that he or she can run back to the AJ and demonstrate that you really don't have much a case at all.

Don't fall for this rather obvious ploy. Your deposition can't be summed up in one question. If it could, why did you spend 2-3 hours answering questions in the first place? Therefore, in this case, feel free to refuse to answer the question. Instead, simply inform the agency attorney that the case is far too complex to be summarized in a single response, but that you would be more than happy to answer questions about any specific area that he or she may be unclear about.

Questions That Call For Speculation

Some questions will make you guess. You don't have to guess. You don't know, for instance, what other people are thinking – unless they tell you, and even then you only know what they tell you, and not what they are really thinking. If you are asked for information you don't know, you can state that it will require you to speculate. This is not the same, however, as testifying to a reasonable inference from a known fact, or to hearsay – both of which are permissible.

Questions That Breach a Privilege

You don't have to answer questions that are protected by a privilege. The most common privileges invoked are attorney-client and doctor-patient, but there are others. If you are asked about conversations that you had with an attorney about your case, you can refuse to answer on the grounds of 'attorney-client privilege.' If you are asked questions about your doctor's medical diagnosis, that is not privileged. If you are asked about conversations you had with your doctor, and advice given, those discussions could be privileged. However, if you are claiming mental anguish and compensatory damages for your mental anguish, many agencies will fight hard to get the maximum amount of information. You can usually be successful in not fighting the release of relevant medical documentation, such as doctor's notes and prescriptions and bills, or allowing your doctor to be deposed as a fact and/or expert witness, and instead fighting the agency's inevitable inquiries into what was discussed.

On that same note, some agencies will try to schedule you for a mental examination. Don't overreact. Research the case law on mental exams, the need for them and what can be done with them. Take a witness along, and be honest. It usually shows the agency is nervous about losing the case and wants to limit its damages. In fact, many cases settle right after a mental exam, when the agency realizes it is in deep trouble not only on liability, but also on the issue of damages.

Argumentative Questions

A final category of objectionable questions is argumentative questions. Now, please understand that, in one sense, all of the agency attorney's questions are argumentative. After all, unlike the counselor or the investigator, the purpose of the agency attorney isn't just to gather the facts. His or her job is to represent the agency and do as much damage to your credibility as possible.

Therefore, with the exception of the first set of questions dealing with your name, age, date of birth and the like, expect the agency attorney's questions to be somewhat argumentative. Yet, some agency attorneys cross the line and ask questions that are not only argumentative, but downright offensive.

For example, in a sexual harassment case, a particularly aggressive agency attorney might ask something like: "Well, coming to the office dressed like a tramp each day, what did you expect?" The only purpose for a question like that is to upset you and put you on the defensive. The hope is that, in your anger, you will say something damaging to your case, or at least, come off sounding like a raving lunatic.

Don't take the bait. Take a deep breath, count to ten, and then calmly refuse to answer the question. "Counselor, this question not only assumes unsubstantiated facts (that I dressed like a tramp), but it is argumentative and quite honestly I find it offensive. Could you please restate the question?"

Using Notes in Your Deposition

Clients frequently ask if they can bring notes to the deposition and testify from them. The answer is "yes." Notes can be used in a deposition or even at a hearing, to refresh your memory, so long as long as you allow the agency lawyer to view them. Therefore, you should be discreet in what your notes say. You certainly don't want anything in your notes that say, "Don't tell them about ...."

Of course it's better to testify without notes. Yet, if you're afraid that you won't remember everything you're supposed to say, feel free to use them.

On the other hand, if you have a very good visual, like a detailed timeline, use it in your deposition and ask that it be attached as an exhibit to the deposition transcript.

Review of the Deposition Transcript: "Read and Sign"

You have the right to 'read and sign' your deposition transcript. That is, you have the right to read through the written transcription of the questions and answers from your deposition, to ensure that they were accurately written down.

It is absolutely critical that you do <u>not</u> waive reading and signing. That is, even if the court reporter does not offer you the opportunity to 'read and sign,' you should mention (on the record) that you would like to exercise your right to read and sign. You will be given an advance copy of the deposition transcript, which you can read at your leisure and make any corrections that need to be made (both as to grammatical errors and as to substantive changes) to the transcript.

Remember, this transcript will most likely be used by the agency in its Motion for Summary Judgment (which we will discuss shortly) and to impeach you at the hearing. You need to know exactly what is said in the transcript, and that it is absolutely accurate. You will sign an "Addendum" and submit it to the court reporter, who will attach it to the deposition transcript.

Chapter 22

Discovery Disputes

When the discovery process works as it's supposed to, it provides each party an opportunity to learn as many of the facts about the case as is possible. This allows each party to prepare, and to put its best foot forward during the hearing. It also encourages settlements, particularly when discovery demonstrates clearly that the employee was the victim of unlawful discrimination. In that case, the agency is more likely to offer a reasonable settlement than to leave its fate in the hands of the AJ (or later, a jury). On the other hand, if discovery shows that a case is without merit, that will often convince a complainant to settle, or withdraw their case.

Unfortunately, discovery doesn't always work as intended when one of the parties acts stubbornly with regards to sharing information. And there are several grounds upon which one of the parties may refuse to comply with a discovery request.

The proper method for not providing information is to file a timely response to discovery, and to assert an objection in writing. In Appendix D, you will find a sample objection. However, in most cases, it is the agency that objects to discovery, since it usually has so much more to hide. You have to be prepared to fight objections to your discovery and to provide some objections to the agency's discovery. Here are some of the more common objections that can withstand scrutiny.

Overbreadth or Irrelevance

One ground for non-compliance is that the request was overbroad or irrelevant. Neither party in discovery is allowed to go on a "fishing expedition," where they ask for every conceivable piece of information in the hopes of somehow turning up some evidence to support their case. As a general rule, you should be able to clearly articulate *why* you need *each* piece of information you request and *how* that information fits into your claim.

To give an outrageous example, let's suppose you send interrogatories to the agency aimed at your boss, whom you claim is guilty of gender discrimination. In these interrogatories, you ask if he watches the WNBA

(Women's National Basketball Association) on TV, how frequently he watches and with whom he watches. Needless to say, the agency can object to this interrogatory because the information requested appears on its face to not be relevant for the purpose of your dispute.

Of course, most discovery requests aren't as clearly irrelevant. In fact, in some cases, a response may seem irrelevant on its face, but actually be quite relevant. For example, let's suppose you request documents demonstrating the promotion practices of the selecting official for five years prior to your non-selection.

Someone might question why this information is relevant. After all, isn't the issue what happened in *this* case? Yet, the truth of the matter is that this information is quite relevant as it could show an ongoing practice of giving promotions to male employees. In fact, the pattern of promotion practices may be the only evidence available to show that gender was a factor in your non-promotion. Therefore, without those documents, or without the interrogatory response asking for the same information, you would likely lose your case.

Perhaps you could even make the first inquiry (about the WNBA) relevant too, by including an allegation that he constantly stares at women's chests, and comments about how women look great in basketball games on TV. Every case is fact-intensive, and "relevant" (as defined in the Federal Rules of Evidence) is anything that is related to a matter, no matter how remotely, that can prove that a fact is true or not. In other words, be prepared to back up each discovery request (interrogatories, requests for production of records, etc.) with an explanation as to how it is relevant.

Overburdensome

Also, a party may object to a discovery request on the ground that it is overburdensome. For example, if you ask for the production of the personnel file of every current and former employee of the EPA, you're asking for too much. It could take months (or even years) for the agency to pull together these millions of pages of documents. Therefore, such a request will be denied, even if you have a valid reason to review the personnel files of *some* agency employees. Therefore, whenever possible, limit your request to just the documents you *need*.

Repetitious Requests

Another ground for refusing a discovery request is that the request is repetitious. For example, let's suppose that you ask to depose 30 different agency employees, all of whom were witnesses to a particular event. If it is expected that all of these witnesses will give essentially the same testimony, then the agency may argue that it isn't necessary to depose all 30 witnesses. Their testimony will be repetitive. The same objection can be made to documentary requests. If several documents all say the same thing, the agency may object to being forced to produce all of them.

Privileged Information

Finally, in very rare cases, the agency may argue against your discovery request on the grounds that the information is privileged. A classic example of such a denial occurs when the requests involves information that is a matter of national security. In those cases, the agency may not have to honor your discovery request, if doing so would require it to reveal sensitive or classified information.

Protective Orders

If the agency raises a legitimate objection on this ground, ask the AJ to compel the agency to produce the documents, but subject to a protective order. This is an order which forces you to return or destroy the documents following the litigation to make sure that they don't fall into the wrong hands. In that way, you get the information you need to proceed with your case and the agency is still allowed to preserve the confidentiality of the information.

Likewise, there may be certain information that you'd like to keep confidential, such as your health records, the identity of your children, their school schedules and the like. As a result, you may seek to have this information subject to a protective order. On the following pages, you will find a sample of such an order.

Motions to Compel

In a perfect world, the agency will respond fully to your discovery requests and that will be the end of the story. However, once again, we don't live in such a world. As a result, the deadline for discovery may come and go and you still may not have received all of your requested documents, interrogatories or depositions.

EQUAL EMPLOYMENT OPPORTUNITY COMMISSION
BALTIMORE DISTRICT OFFICE

IN THE MATTER OF:]	**Current EEO File No.:**
]	**EEOC 123-45-6789X**
Ive Ben Wronged,]	
]	
Complainant,]	
]	
vs.]	
]	**AGENCY #1-H-234-4567-89**
Daniel Glickman,]	
Secretary, Department of Agriculture,]	**OFO Appeal #01234567**
]	
Agency.]	

<u>**PROTECTIVE ORDER**</u>

The parties hereto having stipulated to the entry of a Protective Order under 29 CFR 1614 et seq and Rule 26(c) of the Federal Rules of Civil Procedure and it appearing that such an Order is necessary and appropriate and will facilitate discovery, IT IS HEREBY ORDERED THAT:

Complainant may designate as "confidential" any documents, responses, electronic data, transcripts, or other information, including Responses to Discovery (hereinafter, **"Confidential Information"**) that is produced to the Agency which:

1.   Relate to health and/or medical issues (whether those of Complainant or others);
2.   Relate to Complainant's children and their school schedule(s); and
3.   Similar material

All Confidential Information produced by Complainant and/or his treating medical sources are confidential and shall be subject to the provisions of this Order.

Documents and information designated Confidential Information in accordance with this Order shall be used solely for the purpose of this action or appeal, and those documents and information, and any information contained therein or reasonably inferred therefrom, shall not be disclosed to any person other than (a) counsel of record to this Order; (b) the Administrative Judge; (c) a medical expert retained by the Agency and (d) the EEOC's Office of Federal Operations. Confidential Information disclosed to any such person shall not be disclosed by him/her to any other person not included within the foregoing subparagraphs (a) through (c) of this paragraph. No such documents or information designated as confidential pursuant to this Order shall be used by any such person for any purpose other than for the preparation or trial of this action.

Within twenty-one days after final termination of this action, including any appeals, the Agency shall (a) return to opposing counsel all originals and copies of confidential documents or documents reflecting Confidential Information and any Confidential Information and (b) certify in writing that the provisions of this paragraph have been complied with.

Any document, exhibit, or transcript designated Confidential Information in accordance with this Order, and which is otherwise admissible, may be used at trial, provided, however, that the parties agree that they will work with the Court to identify trial procedures, such as filing under seal and/or in camera reviews, that will protect and maintain the private nature of highly sensitive information. If filed under seal, the protected information will nevertheless be accessible to the EEOC Office of Federal Operations.

Nothing contained in this Order, nor any action taken in compliance with it, shall operate as an admission or assertion by any witness or person or entity producing documents that any particular document or information is, or is not, admissible into evidence.

Nothing herein constitutes or may be interpreted as a waiver by any party of the attorney-client privilege, attorney work product protection, doctor-patient privilege or any other privilege.

Nothing in this Order shall prevent any party from using or disclosing their own documents or information, regardless of whether they are designated confidential.

IT IS SO ORDERED:

_____
Administrative Judge Samuel Teitelman

AGREED TO:

_____   _____
Michael J. Snider, Esq.   Sam Shelton, Esq.
Snider & Associates, LLC   US Department of the Army
Attorney for Complainant   Attorney for the Agency

In that case, you must be assertive and swing into action. Most AJs will include in their Acknowledgment Order a requirement that before filing a Motion to Compel discovery, the moving party must first make a good faith effort to resolve the matter with the opposing representative, and even file a certificate of compliance with this requirement with the Motion.

Your first step is to contact the agency attorney and find out why the discovery request hasn't been granted or fully answered. Perhaps, the request has been denied because it was overbroad or burdensome. In that case, perhaps you can come to a compromise with the agency attorney that will still preserve the intent of your original request, but not be objectionable. The party answering discovery is supposed to state clearly every ground for objecting to discovery, but you don't always get the full picture of what they *are* willing to provide – only what they are *not* willing to provide.

For example, let's suppose you're bringing a claim for religious discrimination and attempting to prove that no Buddhist ever gets promoted above a certain level in your department. In your original discovery request, you asked for the employment records of *all* employees in your department over the last, say, five years. If the agency complains that this request is overbroad and/or burdensome, perhaps you can compromise by asking for the employment records of all Buddhist employees and those employees who reached beyond the grade ceiling level below which Buddhists are trapped. In that way, you will be able to demonstrate the disparity without overburdening the agency.

If your attempts at compromise fail (and they sometimes will), then the next step is to file a motion to compel with the AJ.

Please note that you **must file** this motion within ten (10) days following the deadline for the agency to respond to your discovery (or whatever the AJ set forth in the Acknowledgment Order). And remember, you can only file this motion *after* attempting to resolve your dispute with the agency. Therefore, you must take immediate action once the discovery deadline passes in order to be able to preserve your rights to discovery.

This is no small point. In fact, many employees lose their cases during this stage of the proceedings. They fail to act quickly in objecting to the agency's failure to produce relevant discovery and find themselves out of luck. And without access to critical information, they're unable to prove their case. Don't let this happen to you! You have a right to discovery, but it's up to you to enforce this right.

You have to attach a copy of your discovery to your Motion to Compel, as well as a copy of the agency's response to your discovery (if there is any) and generally a certificate of good faith effort to resolve the dispute. If the agency is the one filing the Motion to Compel, they are obligated to file the same information and follow the same process.

Once you file the Motion to Compel (a sample of which is provided on the next page), the agency will have ten (10) days to respond with its opposition to the motion (and vice versa). In its opposition, it must state the grounds for its refusal. As we've discussed, the most common allowable grounds are that the request is irrelevant, overburdening, repetitious, or privileged.

In considering your Motion to Compel, the AJ will take each of these factors into account. If the AJ finds that your discovery request was reasonable in light of these restrictions, he or she will order the agency to comply with your request within a certain time period (usually 15 days). Or the AJ may modify your original request so that it fits within the bounds of allowable discovery and order the agency to comply with the revised request.

Many AJs will get the parties on the phone for a brief discussion about the dispute, to try and get more information and perhaps to try and get the parties to resolve the dispute by narrowing the information requested. You need to be very prepared for this discussion – have in front of you the discovery, the ROI and anything else you need to convince the AJ that the information you are seeking is material, relevant and reasonably available to the agency.

Failure to Comply With a Motion to Compel

If a party fails to comply with the AJ's order, then the AJ can impose a variety of sanctions. For one, the AJ can simply decide to infer that the requested information must be favorable to your case. In other words, he or she will give you the "benefit of the doubt" concerning that subject at the hearing. The AJ may also decide to exclude conflicting evidence offered by the agency to contradict this inference. Finally, in some cases, the AJ may even go so far as to rule in your favor on some or all of the issues without the benefit of a hearing.

Once again, discovery is a two-way street. Therefore, you have the same rights as the agency to refuse a discovery request when the information is irrelevant, overburdening, repetitive or privileged. And, likewise, you may be subject to the same sanctions for failing to comply with an order imposed by the AJ, so tread lightly in this respect. If you are the one not providing the information, an adverse inference can be drawn against you, which could end your case or seriously hamstring your attempts to get justice.

U.S. EQUAL EMPLOYMENT OPPORTUNITY COMMISSION
WASHINGTON FIELD OFFICE

IN THE MATTER OF:	]	**Current EEO File No.:**
	]	**EEOC 123-45-6789X**
Ive Ben Wronged,	]	
	]	
Complainant,	]	
	]	
vs.	]	
	]	**AGENCY #1-H-234-4567-89**
Daniel Glickman,	]	
Secretary, Department of Agriculture,	]	**OFO Appeal #01234567**
	]	
Agency.	]	

MOTION TO COMPEL RESPONSES TO DISCOVERY AND FOR SANCTIONS

Complainant respectfully requests that the Agency be compelled to respond to her Discovery and that the Agency be sanctioned.

1. In January 2004, Complainant's counsel filed a Motion for Sanctions and a Request for a Hearing with the EEOC in Washington, DC, which has never been responded to by the Agency (ROI pp 29-34).

2. Complainant's Counsel received the Acknowledgment Order in this case on July 6, 2005.

3. Discovery was filed with the Agency on <u>July 21, 2005</u> (**Attached**).

4. The Agency's Responses to Discovery were due no later than Monday, August 22, 2005. To date, <u>no</u> Response has been received.

5. The Acknowledgment Order states:

> Discovery motions, including motions to compel, must be filed within ten (10) calendar days after receipt of a deficient response or after the response to the discovery is due, whichever occurs first. Motions to compel and other discovery motions must be accompanied by the discovery requests and responses and a declaration stating that the moving party has made a good faith effort to resolve the discovery dispute. The declaration shall indicate the efforts made to resolve the dispute and identify which items remain in dispute. Statements in opposition to discovery motions must be filed within ten (10) calendar days of receipt of the motion. Rulings will be made based upon the written submissions. The failure to timely file objections to discovery may result in the objections being deemed waived.

6.   A timely Motion to Compel would be filed on or before September 1, 2005.

7.   A good faith effort has been made to resolve this dispute. Complainant's counsel emailed the Agency representative on August 30, 2005 at 1:00 a.m. and requested the status of the Agency responses, noting that if responses were not received by COB August 31, 2005, 40 days after service of discovery, a Motion to Compel would be filed.

8.   The Agency's attorney replied, astonishingly, that as of August 31, 2005, she had not received any Discovery request from Complainant.

9.   Of course, Complainant served her Discovery upon the same individual that all other documents had been served, including the Acknowledgment Order; the Motion to Amend the Issue, to Consolidate and for Sanctions; the Order to Show Cause, etc. The fax proof of delivery is attached to the Discovery, annexed hereto.

10.   The Agency has refused to provide responses and has declined to provide any date that it will provide responses to Discovery.

11.   The Agency's failure to provide any responses to Discovery is seriously hampering Complainant's ability to schedule depositions in this case, and to timely complete Discovery within the strict time deadlines contained in the Acknowledgment Order.

Since the Agency has failed to respond to Discovery, and has indisputably and unjustifiably delayed the EEO process, failed to investigate eleven (11) Complaints, failed to process two (2) full-fledged complaints and failed to conduct a proper investigation into the instant Complaint, appropriate sanctions should be levied.

Respectfully Submitted,

_____
Michael J. Snider, Esq.
Ari Taragin, Esq.
Jeff Taylor, Esq.
Snider & Associates, LLC
104 Church Lane, Suite 201
Baltimore, MD 21208
410-653-9060 voice
410-653-9061 fax

Motions in Limine

Sometimes, a party wishes to exclude particular evidence at a hearing, or from consideration by the administrative judge. Of course, this is sort of like 'unringing the bell.' In other words, you can ask the AJ to consider the following argument: "This evidence [X] exists, but we want you to exclude it from all consideration and pretend that it does not exist." This is known as a Motion to Exclude Evidence, or a Motion in Limine.

We had a case in which the agency selected a Caucasian employee over an obviously much more qualified African American employee. The agency claimed that it relied upon 'poor work product' in its rejection of the African American employee, including grammar, punctuation, spelling and other mistakes. In discovery, we requested copies of all documents relied upon to reject the Complainant for the position in question. No documents were provided at all.

We filed a Motion in Limine to exclude any evidence (including testimony) about grammar, punctuation, spelling and other alleged errors by the complainant, since the agency didn't provide any in discovery. Ironically, we also asked for a representative sample of the "glowing work" of the selectee.

You would think that they would have provided only error free work, right? The agency actually chose to hand over ten documents, 8 of which were rife with spelling, punctuation and grammar errors! That showed us that carefully crafted discovery, and careful review of discovery responses, can really help your case.

Chapter 23

Prehearing Statements, Prehearing Conference and Settlement Judges

Witness Lists and the Prehearing Statement

Either in the Acknowledgment Order or in a supplemental Order, administrative judges usually set forth deadlines for submission of a Witness List and Prehearing Statement by each party.

Whether they are submitted as separate documents or together, the Witness List and Prehearing Statement are <u>critical</u> documents that require time and effort to prepare. AJs often require that you set forth, in great detail, every factual allegation that you intend to prove at the hearing, every legal argument that you intend to advance at the hearing, and the name, address, title and detailed testimony of every witness you intend to call at the hearing. If you are claiming compensatory damages, most AJs will require that you set forth in specific detail all facts you are relying upon to prove your compensatory damages, all medical information and all proof of damages, as well as what dollar amount you are seeking and how you arrived at that figure. These are stressful documents to prepare, especially when your life for the last year or two has at least partially revolved around your EEO case.

If you are not detailed enough, the AJ can exclude evidence at the hearing that is not contained in the Prehearing Statement. If your Witness List is not descriptive enough, the AJ can reject a witness for the hearing because it is not clear how relevant the testimony will be.

Often, the agency's Witness List will be overly vague as to what the witnesses are to testify about. You can protest that, and bring it to the attention of the administrative judge. Better yet, you can write a letter to the agency attorney and ask for more detail and, if they refuse, then approach the AJ for help.

Some AJs will allow you to amend your Prehearing Statement once before the hearing. If there is any information that changes, or that comes to your attention prior to the hearing, take advantage of the offer and submit an

Amended Prehearing Statement.

The Prehearing Conference

The vast majority of AJs will schedule a Prehearing Conference, and most of them are held a week or two before the hearing. It is at this meeting (usually held by telephone) that the AJ will rule on all outstanding matters, including discovery disputes and Motions in Limine. The AJ will also rule on who will testify at the hearing as a witness and will discuss the hearing procedures, burden of proof and settlement.

Be Prepared

You should prepare for the Prehearing Conference in advance. Gather all documents that have been filed in the case (Discovery, Responses, Witness Lists, Prehearing Statements, etc.) and organize them well.

Review all proposed witnesses. For your proposed witnesses, be prepared to explain in detail what each witness will testify to, and how it is directly relevant to your case. For instance,

- Will the witness establish a fact that is in dispute?

- Will the witness cast doubt upon the agency's proffered non-discriminatory reasons for its actions?

- Will the witness help establish damages?

- Is the witness going to corroborate your testimony?

- Is the witness needed to lay a foundation for a document that is relevant?

For agency witnesses, be prepared to object if the witness is not directly necessary, or appears to not have relevant information. The agency will have to answer the same questions you had to answer, and you can still object if the agency wants to call more than one witness to say the same thing (i.e., the testimony will be duplicative).

Things to Clarify During the Prehearing Conference

You will want to ask the AJ a few things during the Prehearing Conference, such as whether a witness room will be available, whether they typically take a lunch break (if you have diabetes or other eating issues, raise them now) or allow snacks, whether they allow or want an opening statement, oral closing statement or a brief and other such issues.

You also will want to ask the AJ if the hearing will be "bifurcated." In addition to sounding really smart, you will be asking the AJ whether the hearing will proceed in two parts: 1) liability and 2) damages. You can cut the number of witnesses in half in most cases by first having a hearing on whether you win or not, and only then having a hearing on how much you deserve as damages. There are other reasons to bifurcate a case, such as saving some up-front money on an expert damages witness, or saving yourself and family members from having to necessarily testify to heart-rending damages. That is because in many, many cases, if you prevail on liability, the agency will get much more serious about settlement. In fact, many cases are settled between the liability and damages hearings.

Settlement Discussions during the Prehearing Conference

Many administrative judges engage the parties in settlement discussions during the Prehearing Conference. Be prepared to discuss concrete (and reasonable) settlement terms. Be creative in coming up with a proposal, a fall-back position and alternative relief.

"Ex Parte" Discussions

You can ask to speak to the AJ "ex parte," or without the other party present, which will often give you an opportunity to be perfectly frank with the AJ. Of course, if you get the chance to talk to the AJ alone, so will the other side – and you never know what mud they sling during that time.

Settlement Techniques

Some people believe that you need to be "reasonable" during settlement discussions. Reasonable, however, is in the eye of the beholder. If you have a good case on liability, and the only issue is going to be "how much," you will be in a stronger position to negotiate. If the agency wants a "gag clause," where you cannot tell anyone about the settlement agreement, you may be able to squeeze more out of them. Don't start at $300,000, because that will be labeled a "high ball" offer and you will get back (appropriately) a "low ball" offer.

Many administrative judges will ask the parties if they would like to have a settlement conference before a Settlement Judge (often another AJ from the same office). The Washington DC and Baltimore, MD Hearings Offices have formal Settlement Judge programs, which have proven very successful in resolving complaints.

Settlement Conferences

A settlement conference can differ greatly from the AJ's settlement discussions during the Prehearing Conference. For one, the Settlement Judge (if there is one) is supposed to act more like a mediator. A mediator will generally have a very brief meeting between the parties, all together in one room, for an introduction, discussion of the ground rules and perhaps to get the initial positions of the parties out in the open. Then each party will go to a separate room and the mediator will shuttle back and forth, or the mediator stays in the room and each party goes out one at a time. It can be time consuming, but mediation is a proven method of settling cases.

We have come to the conclusion that a good mediator will make both sides unhappy. If both sides are unhappy, you have a good settlement. That is tongue-in-cheek, of course, but it also means that the mediator hasn't favored one side over the other, hasn't made statements negatively about either side's case in front of the other side, and has generally acted (and been perceived as being) even-handed.

What is said behind closed doors, during one-on-one sessions with each party, is supposed to remain totally confidential. You can share information with a mediator / Settlement Judge that you do not want the other side to ever know about (like your fears of staying in your position, your "bottom line" or the fact that you really don't want monetary relief at all, and would settle for a retirement package).

A skillful intermediary will find out quickly where the middle ground is between the parties, and slowly move them together. An unskilled Settlement Judge will keep the parties together in the same room, make comments about the merits of the case, and leave the settlement conference wondering why the case didn't settle.

Prehearing Exchange of Documents

Assuming that settlement and mediation fail, most AJs will require that the parties exchange all documents they intend to introduce at the hearing.

Be thorough and very careful to include *all* documents. The ideal method is to assemble your documents in the order that they will be testified about (i.e., Witness #1 will testify about Complainant's Exhibits ("CX") 1-4; Witness #2 will testify about CX 5-15, etc.). Every AJ has a different method, though, so you should clarify that with them beforehand. Some like exhibits to be pre-marked. Others like them to be marked at the time they are introduced at the hearing. Some like you to use letters, some like you to use numbers and some could care less.

Once you have assembled all of your documents, copy at least four (4) packages and insert clearly numbered tabs so anyone can flip directly to the exhibit you will be asking questions about. Try not to combine documents into one exhibit, and if the exhibit is more than a few pages, you should number them (be sure to number them on the original before you copy them, otherwise you run the risk of having different pages with different numbers). One package is for the agency; one is for the administrative judge, one for the witness and one for you (or your representative). Some AJs want an extra package for the court reporter, so it pays to be prepared for that as well.

Documents Being Used Solely For Impeachment

One tip that many people don't know about is that you don't have to exchange documents which will be used "solely for impeachment." That is a term of art, and you have to watch out for it. To "impeach" means to show someone is not being credible (i.e., they are lying). For instance, in a sexual harassment case, you can ask an agency witness if they ever sent any pornographic emails to co-workers. If they say that they have, then you don't need to impeach them – they admitted the truth. If they say that they have not, then you can whip out a copy of the pornographic email and "impeach" them (i.e., show that they were not telling the truth).

Documents Being Used Solely To Refresh Recollection

Another document you don't have to exchange is one that will be used solely to refresh a witness's recollection. If they claim they cannot recall (it is ironic how many witnesses lose their memories on the stand), then you can use a document to refresh their recollection, and you don't have to enter that into evidence either. You do, however, have to show it to the agency attorney before you show it to the witness. If the agency objects, simply tell the AJ that you are not entering the document into evidence – you are merely using it to refresh the witness's memory.

Chapter 24

Summary Judgment

With the conclusion of discovery and after the Prehearing Conference, there is only one technical obstacle left before moving directly to the hearing – summary judgment. Very often, the agency will file a Motion for Summary Judgment ("MSJ," also called a Motion for Decision Without a Hearing) with the AJ before the hearing. In its motion, the agency will claim that there are no material issues in dispute and as a matter of law, the AJ must rule in favor of the agency. In other words, the agency will claim that, even if *everything* you allege is true, you simply don't have a case and you cannot win.

Extensions of Time, Responding to Agency MSJ

In this situation, you usually have 15 days from receipt of the motion to file an opposition to summary judgment. If you need an extension of time, ask for one right away (first ask the agency if there is any opposition to an extension, and then file a Motion with the AJ). In your Opposition, you must either argue that there are indeed material facts in genuine dispute which must be resolved at the hearing, or (less frequently) that there are no material facts in dispute, but that the AJ must rule in *your* favor as a matter of law.

Of course, as we have explained, even if there aren't material facts in dispute, this doesn't mean that you've automatically lost your case. In fact, it might be just the opposite. If it's clear from the facts that you've been the victim of unlawful discrimination, then the AJ can dispense with a hearing and simply rule in your favor. To obtain this result, you simply file your own Motion for Summary Judgment. In this case, the agency has 15 days to file a motion in opposition to your Motion for Summary Judgment. Sometimes it makes more sense for you to file your motion first, and other times it is strategically better to wait until the agency has filed and for you to file a Cross-Motion for Summary Judgment.

Decision without a Hearing

Interestingly, in some cases, the AJ will save both parties the trouble of filing motions and counter motions and simply decide on his or her own that a hearing isn't necessary. In such a case, however, the AJ <u>must</u> give the parties notice of his or her intent to issue a decision without a hearing, and give both parties the opportunity to file briefs on the issue of whether there is a genuine dispute of fact.

It's important to remember that the only purpose of the hearing is to allow the AJ to weigh conflicting evidence. Therefore, if you have one witness that says one thing and the agency has another witness that says the opposite, the AJ will want to hear from these parties at the hearing and make his or her own determination about the credibility (or knowledge) of these witnesses. That assumes that the testimony in conflict is regarding a material fact and not some collateral issue. However, when there are no material facts in dispute, a hearing is unnecessary.

Definition of "Material Facts"

By the way, for this purpose, the term "material facts" means facts essential to the outcome of the case. Obviously, if the only matters up for dispute are the color of your suit on the day in question or whether it was rainy or sunny on that day, this is not a dispute about a material fact. The dispute must center around some issue that would have an impact on the AJ's ultimate ruling.

For example, if you claim that the agency had an unwritten policy of not giving overtime opportunities to Native Americans and the agency disagrees with this assertion, then this is a dispute over a material fact. Of course, this is provided that your claim is that you've been discriminated against based upon your Native American heritage. On the other hand, if your claim is for age bias, the agency's policy of racial discrimination isn't material to *your* particular claim.

The "Material Facts" Must Be In "Genuine Dispute"

Presenting enough material facts to the AJ won't be enough – *how* you present them will matter as well. There must be a "genuine dispute" over the material facts, not something else. There is not a lot of case law on what is a "genuine dispute," but there is clear EEOC OFO case law that says that conflicting sworn affidavits definitely qualify as a "genuine dispute."

Getting past summary judgment is a major hurdle in all litigation and administrative hearings are no exception. However, if there are truly disputes on material issues of fact, then the AJ will likely allow your case to proceed to the hearing.

Limited Scope of Hearing

In many cases, however, the AJ will limit the scope of the hearing to include just those issues in dispute. As a result, while you may have been planning on calling four witnesses to make your case, the AJ may decide that two of your witnesses are unnecessary and only allow you to call the remaining two.

If this happens, you shouldn't become discouraged. In fact, you should actually be emboldened. In limiting the scope of the hearing, the AJ is essentially telling you that you've convinced him or her as to the potential merit of your case on that particular issue. This can be very good news.

Besides, whenever your case makes it to the actual hearing, you should consider yourself ahead of the game. Sadly, most EEO claims don't make it this far. Also, if you've survived a Motion for Summary Judgment, then it means that you may have a case. It also means that you stand a decent chance of winning, so long as your evidence is more convincing than the agency's evidence at the hearing.

Defeating Summary Judgment

We wish there was a magical recipe to include here which would guarantee that any reader could defeat a Motion for Summary Judgment. Unfortunately, it isn't that simple. Creating a "genuine dispute of material fact" takes time and planning. 15 days is not a lot of time to do legal research, collect exhibits, write a brief and make all of the copies necessary. You can use your Prehearing Statement as the starting point for your Motion or Opposition to Motion for Summary Judgment, but a critical element of your motion or opposition is sworn affidavits from yourself, and from favorable witnesses.

The nice thing about an affidavit (as opposed to deposition or hearing testimony) is that *you* get to say exactly what the testimony will be, what words are used and the way they are presented. Obviously you cannot get (and should not ever attempt to get) a witness to sign a "sham affidavit," but you can use certain phrases and words in witness affidavits that will go a long way towards helping your case. You want to use strong wording, factual content and clear conclusions.

You should put your own affidavit in evidence and even a new affidavit if the ROI affidavit is at all unclear. Now is when you can attach helpful affidavits from witnesses that the investigator overlooked (or intentionally didn't interview). You can (and should) also attach to your opposition any evidence that you want the AJ to consider in ruling on the Motion for Summary Judgment.

In the next chapter, we're going to show you how to present your evidence in the hearing in such a way so that you clear this last hurdle to victory.

Chapter 25

The Hearing

Assuming that your case has survived summary judgment (or that the AJ has not already ruled in your favor), the next step is have your "day in court." Now, before getting into the specifics of how to present your case, we would like to remind you that you do have the right to be presented by an attorney or non-attorney representative at the hearing. This is important to remember because, let's face it, not everyone has the ability or inclination to be a good advocate. It is also hard to ask yourself questions (if you are going to be a witness), so you may have to bring along a friend to ask you questions, unless the AJ will allow you to testify in a monologue.

It's important to remember that, at this point in the process, your entire claim will rest upon whether you make a showing at the hearing that your version of the facts is more credible than the agency's version of the facts. In other words, you must be able to put together a <u>more convincing</u> case than your employer. If you're a normally reserved and quiet person, you may be at a disadvantage in this regard.

In fact, even if you are a regularly outspoken and convincing person, you may still be at a disadvantage in terms of experience. You must remember that your boss and co-workers will not be representing themselves at the hearing. They will be represented by a trained professional who specializes in these types of hearings. That's a considerable advantage for the agency. Often the agency brings *two* attorneys (there's strength in numbers, right?), which can be very intimidating.

Therefore, you may wish to consider offsetting this advantage by enlisting the aid of a competent attorney who specializes in this area of the law. That being said, we've written this book to help you fight your own battle in this regard. Therefore, in this chapter, we'll explain how to go it alone.

The Opening Statement

Some AJs will request, or at least allow, a brief opening statement. Your opening statement is by nature an argument. It should be, however, very factual and have a few case citations thrown in. You can ask the AJ during the Prehearing Conference if he or she allows or wants an opening statement. If you are allowed to deliver one, don't give up that opportunity. Put it in writing and make enough copies for the AJ, the agency, the court reporter and yourself. You can read it into the record, but be sure to review it before hand and to read it out loud – even to a friend, for practice.

The opening statement is a roadmap for your case. It tells the AJ what evidence you will introduce to support your case, and that the agency witnesses will prove to be not credible. You might not want to show your entire hand at this point on your cross examination of the agency witnesses, but you can give the AJ a heads up that their credibility will be seriously questioned.

Your opening statement and closing argument (whether oral or in writing in the form of a brief) are the bookends between which all of the evidence is sandwiched – make them count.

The Credibility Contest

The important thing to remember is that the hearing is usually just a credibility contest. After all, the AJ has already heard your side of the story. He or she has also heard the agency's side of the story. In resolving the inconsistencies between the two, the AJ is going to have to make a judgment call about the credibility of your respective witnesses. Or, in other words, he or she is going to have to determine whose witnesses are most likely relating the events as they *actually* happened. It really comes down to a battle of credibility.

So how do you establish credibility for yourself and your witnesses? Well, take a look at the statement below written by an AJ in a case where the complainant lost. The AJ says it very succinctly,

> *"Clearly, I do not believe Complainant and I found his testimony to be non-credible in this and other regards. Complainant's manner and appearance during his testimony, as well as his frequent evasiveness, inconsistency, and resort to innuendo and hyperbole, affected my ability to believe him."*

To establish credibility, a witness must, at the very least, be able to provide direct and exact answers to the questions posed. Of course, it always helps to be able to provide corroborating witnesses, documents and other evidence to bolster your credibility. However, remember, if the AJ doesn't believe you (or your witnesses), that is already two strikes against you.

Types of Witnesses

At the hearing, you will generally be calling two types of witnesses: (1) fact witnesses and (2) experts. Your fact witnesses will be those people who were present at the time of the event and saw or heard what happened, or who have relevant hearsay (which is admissible) about which they can testify.

Fact Witnesses

For example, if the purpose of the hearing is to determine whether your boss made a certain inappropriate remark, you would want to call a person who overheard the remark and is willing to testify truthfully on your behalf, or someone who heard the boss later talking about making the remark, or someone who heard you accuse him of making the remark and saw him not refute it.

Other types of fact witnesses are those needed to 'authenticate' a document (i.e., testify that it is genuine) and damages witnesses (those who can testify to the effect the discrimination had upon you). In an Equal Pay Act case, you will want to use a witness who has observed you performing the same work as a higher-paid employee of the opposite gender. The ideal testimony would be from the higher-paid employee(s) themselves, who could also testify about what they do and how they do it.

Expert Witnesses

On the other hand, expert witnesses are those who have a demonstrated expertise that's relevant to the case at hand. These people don't testify as to what they saw or heard, but rather they testify as to what they *know*.

For example, let's suppose that your boss failed to allow you to participate in a training program because you were pregnant at the time. The agency doesn't dispute this fact but rather claims that the discrimination was not a "tangible employment action," as the denial of this training opportunity didn't do you any actual harm on the job. To rebut this assertion, you may have to call a government classification specialist to support your claim that the loss of training opportunities would be viewed by management as a serious strike against you in a future promotion decision. As you can see, this person wouldn't be testifying as to any interaction he or she witnessed between you and your boss, but rather about his or her knowledge of promotion decisions in the agency.

Another type of expert witness is someone with subject matter expertise. In an earlier example, we told you about a USPS employee who was very sensitive to cold temperatures. She claimed that the air conditioning blew on her and she needed accommodation in the form of a space heater and cubicle walls. The agency claimed that it was nice and warm and toasty in the facility. We used an expert on HVAC systems to testify about the air conditioning and output temperatures. In general, disability discrimination cases are good candidates for expert witnesses, and you can recover expert witness fees as part of your recovery if you win.

One good tip is that, since expert witnesses can be expensive, you might be able to save some money by searching around your agency for someone who could testify as an expert, but whom you wouldn't have to pay to do so. For instance, many federal agencies have HVAC experts, medical doctors, psychologists and nurses on staff. If you are able to talk to them, you can enlist them in your case and qualify them (by way of their credentials) as an expert, while saving yourself some up-front money.

Choosing Witnesses

In choosing your witnesses, the first criterion is obviously their willingness and ability to testify for you. Needless to say, the former co-worker who has retired to Tahiti isn't likely to fly several thousand miles for your hearing (of course, they may be willing to testify by phone or videoconference, both of which are becoming more popular in EEO hearings).

Also, in some cases, you will have to deal with a reluctant witness. This person may still be employed with the agency and may not wish to contradict the testimony of a boss or co-worker for fear of retaliation.

Ironically, this is just the person you usually *want* to testify on your behalf – the reluctant witness. The truth of the matter is that the reluctant witness appears simply more credible than the witness who has an obvious vendetta against his or her former boss or co-workers. For this reason, you want to use every effort to convince the reluctant witness to do the right thing – testify truthfully at the hearing. Many federal employees will open up once put under oath (while others, including some management, will make outright lies despite the oath).

If the witness won't cooperate in this regard, please remember that you have the right to request the AJ to compel the witness to attend and provide his or her testimony. However, this power is limited. The AJ only has the power to compel some current federal employees to testify. Of course, a request to compel a witness to attend should be a last resort and only employed when all efforts at persuasion have failed.

On the matter of logistics, it is up to the agency attorney(s) to actually arrange for the presence of agency employees at the hearing. The agency attorney may have to work with other federal agencies to get their employees to attend. If you have a witness who is retired or is a private employee, it is your responsibility to make sure they are available to testify and present at the hearing (or by phone, if the AJ allows it). You can confirm with the AJ at the Prehearing Conference as to the method of testimony (e.g., in-person, phone, or video) is acceptable.

Presenting Your Witnesses: Direct Examination

As the complainant, you have the burden of proof and therefore, you have to go first. You will need to call your witnesses in a logical order (although you have the right to testify after all of your other witnesses have testified). Usually the AJ will sequester witnesses, which means that only one witness will be in the room at a time. Witnesses are told to not discuss their testimony with anyone outside of the hearing room.

Typical testimony is given in a question and answer format: you ask the witness a question and they answer the question. In direct examination (your questioning of your own witnesses), you are not allowed to use "leading" questions. You are only supposed to use "non-leading" questions. Non-leading questions are those that begin:

- Who ...

- What ...

- Where ...

- When ...

- Why ...

- How ...

No "Leading" Questions Allowed on Direct Examination

Leading questions are those that can be answered "yes" or "no." Leading questions are great (and expected) for cross-examination (which we will cover soon), but not for direct examination. Direct examination is supposed to flow, and you will do best by covering issues chronologically or in some other logical order.

The AJ may give you (as a non-attorney) some leeway in regard to leading questions, but the long and short of it is that you are expected to prepare your witnesses before the hearing. You are expected to go over their testimony with them, and they should know the question you will ask and the answer that is expected of them. You can also object to the agency using leading questions on their direct examination of agency witnesses, but not for using leading questions when they question your witnesses.

One phenomenon we have noticed is that some inexperienced agency attorneys will use open-ended questions for their witnesses, then they will object to the use of leading questions of their witnesses on cross examination. Of course, there is nothing wrong with using leading questions in cross examination, but it catches them by surprise if they are not seasoned. Then, the agency attorney will try to use leading questions on "re-direct" questioning of agency witnesses, which is just as bad as using them during direct questioning. You should object, and the AJ will uphold your objection.

You will, in addition to introducing facts through testimony, want to introduce documents at the hearing as well. There is a method to doing this, which we will now discuss.

Introducing Documentary Evidence

If you have done your job properly, you will have a nice fat ROI with lots of documents in it that you want to use at your hearing. Remember that in 99% of cases, all documents in the ROI are "pre-admitted" into evidence. "Into evidence" means that the AJ can consider them as genuine and relevant to the case. If a document is <u>not</u> in the ROI, then it has to be entered into evidence.

A second method of avoiding entering documents into evidence at the hearing is to use requests for admissions (or to work out a stipulation) that ask the agency to admit or stipulate that the documents you wish to introduce are 1) relevant and 2) genuine. You can always tell them that the AJ hates disputes over documents and you would like to work together to avoid having to argue in front of the AJ. That usually helps soften them up a bit.

If you haven't gotten a document pre-admitted, you will need to "move it into evidence" at the hearing. In order to do that, you should memorize the following script:

- [Show the document to the witness and state:]

- "I have provided you Complainant's Exhibit 1, marked for identification purposes. Do you recognize this document?"

- [Answer, hopefully, is 'yes.']

- "How do you recognize the document?]

- [Answer: I wrote it / received it / etc.]

- "Is this a genuine copy of the document?"

- [Answer, hopefully, is 'yes.']

- "Your Honor, I move Complainant's Exhibit 1 into evidence."

At this point, the AJ will ask the agency if it has any objection to the document and, absent an objection, note that the exhibit is accepted into evidence. You can then refer to it as Complainant's Exhibit 1 throughout the rest of the hearing and in your brief.

Documents Used Solely For Impeachment

As we discussed in a prior chapter, you don't usually have to disclose documents pre-hearing that are used solely for impeachment purposes. These may be 'smoking gun' documents, or other juicy emails or notes. You may have had to disclose them in Discovery, and if you did not you may still be able to use them for limited purposes at the hearing. Since you might want to introduce them into evidence, however, it is best to err on the side of caution and to produce them (perhaps in the middle of a giant stack of other, irrelevant, documents).

Cross Examining Agency Witnesses

Of course, presenting your side of the story is only half the battle. The other half of the battle is to discredit the agency's witnesses. You can do this in one of two ways.

The first way is to demonstrate that the witness is simply mistaken about the facts. The other way is to attempt to demonstrate that the witness may have a motive for being less than truthful. Through the effective use of questions, you can accomplish each of these objectives.

In our experience, there are three rules to effective cross examination:

1. Ask only leading questions.

2. Ask only questions to which you know the answer.

3. Use only one fact per question.

Don't get angry, don't lose control. You are the one in the driver's seat during cross examination. If the witness is evasive, ask the AJ to order them to answer the question. There is <u>nothing</u> more satisfying than having the power to force a high-level federal agency SES-er to answer *your* questions (other than winning, of course). Also, don't get into any arguments with agency counsel. In fact, during the hearing you should rarely, if ever, even address the agency attorney, rather all of your comments, questions, objections and remarks should be directed to the AJ.

There are many great books out there on cross examination, and we have provided a reading list at the end of this book of ones that we have found useful.

Making and Responding to Objections

Previously, we have discussed some types of objections that can be lodged in discovery, like relevance. Similarly, you can raise an objection during the hearing.

Objections Relating to Testimony

The proper way to raise an objection is to wait until the other side has asked a question that you consider objectionable, and then to state out loud to the AJ (before the witness answers): "Your Honor, I object to the question on the grounds that it is [leading, irrelevant, without foundation, vague, outside the timeframe, etc.]". The agency will have a chance to respond, and the AJ will make a ruling – sometimes without explaining the ruling.

If the ruling is to overrule the objection, that means that the AJ will allow the question to be asked, and the AJ will tell the witness to answer. If the AJ agrees with you, he or she will say that the objection is "sustained" and the agency attorney will have to ask a different question, or will have to rephrase the question.

Sometimes the AJ will not make a ruling of overruled or sustained, but will just direct the questioner to "rephrase" the question. This can be exasperating if you don't understand what the objection was to begin with, because you won't understand how to rephrase the question to make it not objectionable any more. Some AJs will step in and ask the witness questions on their own; others will not.

The agency will make objections during your questioning. Sometimes, the objections are well grounded, and other times, they just do it to throw off your rhythm. Don't let them get you riled. You probably have your questions written out in advance anyway, so just get back into the flow. If you don't remember your last question, you can have the court reporter read it back to you.

When the agency objects to your questioning of a witness, don't address your response to the agency attorney. Address it to the AJ. If you don't understand the objection, ask the AJ for clarification.

Objections Relating to the Introduction of a Document

Just like questions in oral testimony can be objectionable (because the matter inquired about is irrelevant or the question is leading), an objection can be lodged against the introduction of a document as well.

The proper time to object to a document is not when it is marked as an exhibit, or even when it is first shown to the witness. You should not generally object to a document until the agency "offers it into evidence." Likewise, if the agency objects to your document when you first hand it to the witness, you can smile knowingly at the AJ and calmly reply, "Your Honor, I have not yet moved it into evidence." The AJ will appreciate your control, as well as your knowledge of the rules of evidence, and instruct you to proceed.

If you do want to object to a document, the grounds are fairly limited. You can object that a "lack of foundation" exists for the document – in other words, that the agency has not proven that the document is genuine. To introduce any document, you need to "lay a foundation." In other words, you need to show that the witness knows about the document, that the document is genuine and that it is relevant to the proceedings. For example, if the case is about a performance appraisal for the period 10/1/03 to 9/30/04, any document from after 10/1/04 will usually be irrelevant.

The "Best Evidence" Rule

Sometimes a witness will start testifying about a document that does not exist, or that you have not been provided. You should immediately object based upon the "best evidence rule," which states that the best evidence is the document, not testimony about it, and that if the agency cannot provide the document, it cannot use testimony about the document either, except in limited circumstances.

There are many, many other rules of evidence that we will not delve into here. If you want to audit a course in trial practice or evidence at your local law school, you may find it interesting and useful.

Practice Makes Perfect

Now, we realize that we've just introduced some concepts that may be new to you. However, please try not to be intimidated. You can really become quite proficient in presenting your case, if you're willing to prepare yourself thoroughly and practice before the hearing. Practice cross-examining a friend or just practice in the mirror. Remember, the better prepared you are, the more comfortable you will feel in the hearing. And believe it or not, your confidence will go a long way towards convincing the AJ that your side of the story is the truth.

Hearing Demeanor

Another important factor in making a good impression is to act appropriately in the hearing. First and foremost, you should be respectful of the administrative judge. You should also be respectful to the court personnel and even, your adversaries. You want to give the impression that you are a reasonable and stable individual; the kind of person who would never bring a claim unless it were indisputably true.

Besides, if you become too unruly, you may be removed from the hearing. This would be bad enough if you were represented by counsel, but it's almost fatal to your case if you're the one representing yourself at the hearing. Therefore, you must refrain from interrupting witnesses when they are testifying; even if their testimony is less than truthful. You simply will not help your case by standing up and yelling, "That's a lie!" During cross-examination, you will have your chance to cast doubt upon their claims.

In a similar fashion, you want to avoid name-calling and making personal attacks. This may seem obvious, but it's easier said than done. This is particularly true when the witness is someone who has just offered unflattering testimony about you. For example, the witness may have just testified that you were an unproductive employee. Or he or she may have even expressed doubts about your character and propensity for telling the truth. In this case, it's only natural to want to verbally lash out at such a person.

Resist the temptation. Remember, you want to demonstrate to the judge that you are a person of integrity and that you are too big of a person to allow emotions or hurt feelings to cloud your judgment. In taking the high road, you further impress the AJ that you are not the type of person who would pursue this matter just to "get even." Besides, name-calling and personal attacks won't likely be allowed anyway and could get you removed from the hearing, so why risk it?

Another important thing to do is to stay on task. You should have a very clear agenda of what you are trying to achieve and you should stick to that agenda. Don't get sidetracked by non-important issues. You may have disagreed with *everything* the opposing witness had to say, but in your cross-examination, you should only address those issues that are pertinent to your case. For example, the fact that the witness falsely claimed that you had a tardiness problem has nothing to do with your sexual harassment case, so let it be.

In this chapter, we have shown you how to present your case in the best possible light at the hearing. There are many, many good books on hearings and trials, but the very best way to learn how to do a hearing is to actually put on a hearing. You can volunteer as a non-attorney representative for other federal employees in their EEO hearings, and put on one or two. If you prefer to not take on that level of responsibility, you can "second chair" a hearing with an attorney or someone else, so you can get your feet wet without endangering someone's case.

Remember, that even if you do have a valid claim for discrimination, unless the AJ believes the evidence presented before him, your claim will fail. So please do your utmost to follow the advice that we have laid out in this chapter. With proper preparation, good documents and believable witnesses, you will hopefully prevail in your pursuit of justice in the workplace.

Chapter 26

The Post-Hearing Brief

At the conclusion of the hearing, you will usually be allowed to file a closing brief that reiterates your position for the AJ (you can clarify this at the Prehearing Conference). While you will not be *required* to write such a brief, it's always a good idea to make things as easy as possible for the AJ to rule in your favor. In writing this brief, you should attempt to summarize the important facts uncovered during the investigation and the hearing and explain how those facts interact with the law to prove your case for unlawful discrimination.

Now, we understand that unless you've had a lot of experience writing these types of briefs, the thought of setting forth your case in writing might seem daunting. However, this is a skill that can be learned with some practice. To help you in drafting your closing brief, we've provided a sample of a brief we drafted for a client in a "reverse discrimination" non-selection case (see Appendix E).

In drafting your brief, be sure to include a section summarizing the important facts in the case – including careful citations to the exact page in the transcript where helpful or critical testimony is located, and a discussion about all of those documents that are in the ROI and your exhibits. Also, spend time explaining why the agency's theory of the case is not valid, why their witnesses are not credible and why their documents are not relevant. You should be provided official time to write your brief, as you should get official time for all of your EEO case work.

Chapter 27

The Administrative Judge's Decision

While most of the EEO complaint and hearing process is filled with rigid deadlines, there is no such deadline for the AJ to issue his or her ruling. In order to keep his or her caseload moving along, an AJ may issue a decision fairly quickly after a hearing. On the other hand, AJs have been known to take a year or more to rule on a case.

Most rulings are issued by mail, although an increasing number of AJs are now setting up conference calls to issue telephonic rulings. In this situation, both parties and a court reporter listen in as the judge issues his or her ruling by phone. In most cases, a telephonic ruling will be followed up with a written decision, which is usually just a marked-up copy of the telephone transcript. This is sometimes called a "bench decision."

And while ideally the AJ's ruling should fully set forth his or her conclusions regarding credibility of witnesses and the legal basis for the ruling, this isn't always the case. In fact, some AJs have been known to rule for summary judgment by simply slapping a one-line letter on the front of the prevailing party's Motion for Summary Judgment or post-hearing brief reading something like, "I accept the Motion of the Agency as my Decision." In our opinion, this type of ruling is an insult and should be appealed almost without reservation (unless it is you that won, of course).

Ruling On Damages and Bifurcation

In addition to determining whether you were the victim of unlawful discrimination, the AJ may also determine the form of your relief; whether you are entitled to monetary damages, attorney's fees, a promotion, reinstatement or other relevant relief. However, in some instances your case may be bifurcated, where the AJ will make separate rulings on the case and the damages involved should you prevail.

In cases where the determination of damages can be tricky, some AJs will decide to schedule two separate hearings. The first hearing will determine whether or not you were the victim of unlawful discrimination. If you win that hearing, then the next hearing will determine your damages. The purpose of bifurcation is judicial economy. After all, why have everyone go through the trouble of calling expert witnesses to determine damages if there hasn't been any unlawful discrimination in the first place?

Finally, in some cases, after the AJ has issued a ruling, he or she will encourage the parties to attempt to settle their dispute one more time. And they often do, because as you will see in the next chapter, the battle is only half over, even after the AJ's ruling.

Chapter 28

Agency Final Action

By this point in the process, you've gone through initial counseling, the investigation period and an administrative hearing. However, the AJ's ruling is by no means the last step in the process. Each party still has a number of arrows left in their respective quivers.

As amazing as it may seem, the AJ's decision is not the last word on the subject. The agency still has forty (40) days in which to review the decision and issue its final agency decision (FAD). The FAD will come in one of two forms: (1) the agency will accept the AJ's decision and agree to fully implement it, or (2) the agency will modify the AJ's decision or reject it outright. A decision solely on liability is not immediately appealable, nor is a decision in which the AJ has not yet ruled on attorney's fees or other relief.

Of course, in the case that the AJ has ruled against you, you can almost be certain that the agency will accept the AJ's decision. On the other hand, if the AJ has ruled in your favor, the agency may decide to accept the AJ's decision or it may decide to reject or modify it. If it chooses to reject or modify the AJ's decision, then the agency must simultaneously file an appeal with the EEOC's Office of Federal Operations (OFO) when it issues the FAD.

Once you receive notice of the FAD, you have a few decisions to make. If the AJ rules in your favor and the agency appeals the case to the OFO, you must decide how you will oppose the agency's attempt to have your favorable decision overturned. You may also want to appeal the AJ's decision yourself, even if it was largely in your favor.

For instance, if you disagree with the AJ's calculation of damages or if you feel that you should have been entitled to some additional relief, like a promotion or increase in pay grade, you may wish to appeal the AJ's decision. Likewise, you may wish to appeal if the AJ wrongly dismissed some of your claims prior to the hearing or ruled in your favor on only some of your claims.

On the other hand, if the AJ ruled *against* you and the agency elected to implement the AJ's ruling (no surprise there), then you will most probably want to appeal the AJ's decision.

Also, for whatever reason, the agency may not issue an FAD within the 40-day time period, leaving you in limbo. In this case, if the agency has failed to comply with the AJ's decision, you can notify the agency's EEO Director in writing of the agency's non-compliance. The agency then has thirty-five (35) days to resolve the matter with you in writing. At the end of this time period, if the agency is still in non-compliance and has failed to resolve the matter, you can take the matter to the OFO. All of this can get very technical and complicated, so be sure to consult the EEOC's regulations. They can found at 29 C.F.R. 1614, which is available at www.eeoc.gov.

Of course, you aren't obligated to do any of these things. Once again, at this point in the process, you are free to abandon the EEO process and take your case directly to federal court. Deciding between these two options – an EEOC appeal and a federal lawsuit – can be difficult. Therefore, in the next few chapters, we will explain the process involved in each option and provide you with some additional information to help inform your choice.

Chapter 29

EEOC Appeals

Filing a Notice of Appeal

You take the first step towards your appeal by completing a Notice of Appeal (EEO Form 573), a copy of which you will find in Appendix F. You must file your Notice of Appeal within thirty (30) days of receiving the FAD. As always, meeting the deadline is critically important. If you don't file your appeal in the required time frame, you will likely lose out on your chance to challenge the AJ's decision.

We recommend that you either mail your Notice of Appeal by certified U.S. mail or deliver it in person and request a filing confirmation, so that you can prove that you appealed in a timely manner should your complaint somehow get misplaced (yes, this happens).

Of course, you are free to send your Notice of Appeal via FedEx or UPS. However, be aware that some appellate agencies, like the Federal Labor Relations Commission, consider such services to be "courier services." Therefore, the appeal isn't considered "filed" until it is received (as opposed to the date it's postmarked if sent U.S. mail). This distinction could prove fatal to your appeal if you're like many people who wait until the last day to put your appeal in the mail. When your appeal arrives the next day, it will be considered late and your appeal will be automatically denied, regardless of its merits.

Finally, you can fax your Notice of Appeal to the OFO at (202) 663-7022, but only if its fewer than 11 pages. The drawback to faxing your appeal, however, is that you won't get a receipt confirming that the OFO received it. Therefore, if your fax gets lost in Never Never Land or if the OFO loses it, you may be out of luck. As you can see, the safest courses of action are to hand-deliver your complaint or send it through the U.S. mail, certified with return receipt.

Also, it's important to note that you must furnish the agency with a copy of your Notice of Appeal at the same time it is filed with the Commission. You can address it to the EEO office (the address should be in the FAD, but you can find it in the ROI also) and it is a courtesy to send a copy to the agency lawyer(s) who opposed you at the administrative level.

Once you've filed for your appeal, you have the right to file a brief in support of your appeal within thirty (30) days. If at all possible, you should take advantage of this opportunity. While the people handling your appeal at the OFO will have access to the factual record and transcripts from the hearing, it certainly can't hurt to assist them in understanding your side of the story.

In this brief, you should set forth your reasons for why the AJ's decision was in error. In doing so, you should explain how the AJ got the facts and/or the law wrong. As always, timing is critical here.

Filing Deadlines

To make sure that there is no confusion as to how the various time periods are computed, let's run through a hypothetical example. Let's suppose that you receive the AJ's decision on March 1st. In his decision, the AJ ruled against you and you decide that you want to appeal.

Yet, please note that you can't file your Notice of Appeal immediately. You must wait up to 40 days (until April 10th) for the agency to issue its FAD, in which it will almost certainly agree to "implement" the AJ's decision. If you do not receive the agency's decision by April 10th, then you have 30 days (or until May 10th) to file your appeal.

On the other hand, if you do receive the FAD within the proper time frame, then you only have 30 days from its receipt to file your Notice of Appeal. So for example, let's say you received the FAD on April 5th. You would then have 30 days from that date (May 5th) to file your Notice of Appeal. Incidentally, if that date falls out on either Saturday, Sunday or a legal holiday, the 30-day deadline gets extended to the next non-holiday business day.

Finally, you have an additional 30 days to file a brief in support of your appeal. It's important to keep track of the date you filed your Notice of Appeal so that you don't miss the deadline for filing your brief. This is particularly important because the OFO has a tendency to inadvertently confuse appellants about the filing date of their appeal.

Likely, you will receive an Appeal Acknowledgment Letter from the OFO during this 30-day period. The letter will usually state something like, "This commission acknowledges receipt of your appeal on the date indicated. Any statement or brief in support of your appeal must be submitted to the commission as well as to the agency within 30 days of filing the notice of appeal."

For illustrative purposes, let's suppose that the date of the letter was September 17, 2003. As a result, you might think that you have 30 days from that date to file your brief. However, the filing date for the Notice of Appeal is actually written lower down on the page - under "Filed: 091505." As a result, you don't have until October 17th (30 days from September 17th) to file your brief. You only have until October 15th.

This tiny discrepancy could cause you to lose your right to file a support brief. So make sure you're counting that 30 days from the right date. Remember, your filing date is the date you faxed, hand delivered or postmarked your Notice of Appeal. Of course, it should be noted that the OFO has been known to consider briefs filed well after the deadline, but it's always best to file your brief in time; just in case.

Also, remember to send a copy of your brief to the OFO and to the agency EEO office, with a courtesy copy to the lawyer who opposed you at the hearing. Upon receiving your brief, the agency has twenty (20) days to file a brief in opposition to your appeal.

Of course, if the agency is the party challenging the AJ's ruling, then the situation is reversed, except that the agency doesn't have 30 days from issuing its FAD to file a Notice of Appeal. It must do so simultaneously with issuing the FAD. It then has 30 days to file a brief in support of its appeal and you have 20 days after that to file your brief in opposition.

The Appellate Standards of Review

The first thing to understand is that filing an appeal doesn't give you an opportunity to conduct a "do over." In almost all cases, the OFO is going to make its determination solely based on the existing factual record and the transcripts from the hearing. Generally, you aren't allowed to introduce new evidence.

There are only two exceptions to this general rule. The first exception is when the record requires supplementation to avoid a "miscarriage of justice." For example, if you found out a witness was bribed after you filed your notice of appeal, you can supplement the record by introducing letters, memorandum, affidavits and other documents. However, even in this case, the OFO isn't going to hold another hearing in which you can introduce witness testimony or cross-examine the agency's witnesses. The other exception is for after-acquired evidence, which is rarely available and hard to prove.

In reviewing cases on appeal, the OFO uses two different sets of standards, depending upon the decision being appealed from. If you're appealing from a decision made unilaterally by the agency, then the OFO uses a more stringent standard of review. However, if you're appealing from an AJ's decision, the OFO employs a more limited review.

Review of Final Agency Decisions

In the former case, the OFO will conduct a *de novo* review. In a *de novo* review, the OFO examines the record without regard to the previous determinations of the agency. In other words, it looks at the evidence with a fresh set of eyes and makes it own independent conclusions.

In doing so, the OFO makes two different types of determinations: factual and legal. It first attempts to come to some kind of conclusion as to the facts of the case – what happened, when and to whom? For instance, in a sexual harassment case involving disputed allegations of inappropriate contact, the OFO will review the record to determine who touched whom, when and where. In doing so, it won't give any deference to the agency's view on the reliability of documentary evidence or credibility of conflicting witnesses. The OFO will come to its own conclusions on these matters.

Likewise, the OFO won't depend upon the agency for applying the facts of the case to the law (i.e., making legal determinations). The OFO will judge the facts as it sees them and then make an independent decision based upon its own understanding of how the law fits the facts of the case. This review function is important in this context because very often, agencies are simply mistaken about what's allowed or required under the law.

Review of AJ Decisions

Unfortunately, the OFO takes a different approach when it comes to reviewing decisions reached by administrative judges. Any factual determinations will be reviewed under a "substantial evidence" standard, as opposed to the *de novo* standard. Under the substantial evidence standard, if there is substantial evidence to support the AJ's determination, then the OFO will defer to this determination, even if the OFO would have come to a different conclusion under the circumstances. The only time when the OFO will overturn an AJ's factual findings on appeal is when those findings are completely contrary to the evidence in the record.

As you can probably imagine, this is a very tough standard to meet. This is particularly true in regards to testimony presented at the hearing. As the AJ was present at the hearing and able to view the demeanor of the witnesses, his or her view on their credibility carries a lot of weight. And for purposes of an OFO appeal, the AJ's determination as to whether the agency was acting with discriminatory intent is a factual determination, which will be afforded the same level of deference.

However, not all of the AJ's determinations are given this level of deference. Legal determinations are reviewed under a *de novo* standard. Or, in other words, the OFO will decide for itself whether the AJ made an error in applying the law to the facts of your case (as he or she saw them).

Understanding how the OFO reviews prior decisions is important because it helps you to decide whether to file an appeal, and if so, how to argue your case. For instance, if your contention is that the AJ came to the wrong factual conclusions, you're going to have an uphill battle on appeal under a substantial evidence standard. On the other hand, if you're challenging the agency's factual conclusions, you stand a better chance of success. The same is true in the case where you are challenging legal conclusions, whether made by the agency or the AJ.

That being said, AJ decisions can be overturned. For example, our firm was successful in getting the OFO to overturn an AJ's finding against an employee denied the reasonable accommodation of reassignment. We argued that the AJ got the facts right, but that she blew the legal analysis. The appellate attorneys and commissioners at EEOC's OFO agreed. Therefore, we were able to transform a loss into a victory on appeal, complete with compensatory damages, reinstated leave and attorneys' fees. Of course, it took over 2 ½ years for the OFO to actually issue its decision, but it was worth it.

Our success in this case notwithstanding, appeals of AJ rulings are rarely successful. This is both good and bad news. On the one hand, if the administrative judge rules against you, it's going to be difficult to get the EEOC to overturn that decision. On the other hand, the agency is going to have the same trouble in getting the EEOC to allow it to do anything but fully implement the administrative judge's ruling. Therefore, as you can see, it's imperative to make every effort to present the best possible case at the hearing stage.

Requests for Reconsideration

There is no OFO deadline to render a decision on appeal and the OFO has had a pretty poor track record of ruling timely on appeals; sometimes taking two or more years to do so (although things have improved recently). When the OFO finally issues its ruling, either party may exercise its right to file a second (and final) appeal asking the OFO to reconsider its ruling.

To do so, the appealing party must submit a request for reconsideration and any supporting brief within thirty (30) days of the OFO's decision on the original appeal. Once again, the opposing party then has twenty (20) days to file a brief in opposition.

Needless to say, requests for reconsideration are successful even less often than appeals, although they are usually decided much quicker. After all, the request for reconsideration is, in a sense, like asking the OFO, "Are you sure?"

Nevertheless, this request can be granted in one of two situations: (1) The appellate decision was clearly erroneous; or (2) The decision will have a substantial impact on the policies, practices, or operations of the agency. Of the two options, it is our opinion that appellants have a much better chance of pursuing the first line of reasoning, since the second is really an agency defense to implementing a decision.

And while a request for reconsideration is a long shot, the OFO does reconsider its prior decisions from time to time. That being the case, you might be asking, "Why would anyone utilize this procedure?"

The answer usually comes down to the fact that, by this point, the appellant is already heavily invested into the process, so why not see it through to the end? After all, by the time you reach this stage, you'll probably be more than two years into the process. What's another two or three months to get some closure on the outcome?

Besides, the only other viable option at this stage is to take your case to federal court. And while your chances will certainly increase in this new venue, so will your expenses and the time it will take to reach a resolution. Filing a lawsuit will, in effect, start the entire process over again.

We are aware of at least two cases in which federal employees won their cases before EEOC AJs (and/or the EEOC OFO) and filed a complaint in federal district court seeking even more damages. In both cases, the court required a bond to be posted, in case the judge or jury threw out the case or awarded less in damages. In short, if you win, take the money and run.

Chapter 30

Taking Your Fight to Court

As you can see, the EEO process can drag on for what may seem like forever. At some point, after going through the initial counseling, investigation and hearing, you may feel that you've simply had enough of the whole administrative process. In that case, you may decide that it's time to jump straight to federal court.

As you know, unless your claim is for a violation of the EPA or the ADEA, you can't simply file a civil lawsuit at your discretion. You can only do so at certain prescribed times in the process (e.g., upon completion of the investigation, 180 days after the start of the investigation, etc.). Well, the agency's issuance of the FAD is another opportunity to go "jump ship" on the process and take your battle to federal court.

In fact, in some cases, this may be your last opportunity to avail yourself of the federal courts. Claims made under the EPA and the ADEA can be brought to court directly after the initial act of discrimination. You don't have to undergo so much as an initial interview in order to file a lawsuit. Of course, you are free to utilize the EEO process (and there are many good reasons to do so). Yet, filing an EEOC complaint does not stop the clock on the statute of limitations for those claims.

For example, under the EPA, you must file a lawsuit within three years of the discriminatory action, or you will lose your right to file permanently. Furthermore, in some cases, you'll only be allowed to recover back wages for the two years prior to filing your lawsuit. Therefore, it's important not to get so bogged down in the EEO process that you allow these time periods to lapse and forfeit your right to pursue your claim in federal court.

In many cases, the administrative judge ruling and the resulting final agency decision marks a good time to reassess the EEO process and make a decision whether to "fish or cut bait." In an earlier chapter, we outline a few factors to consider in taking your case to federal court. As a reminder, before making the decision to file a lawsuit, you should consider: (1) your financial situation; (2) the availability of witnesses; and (3) the jury appeal of your case.

The Necessity for Representation

Also, there are a few additional things you should know about the federal civil litigation system. For one, federal court is not the place to go it alone. Unlike the EEOC process, federal civil procedure is not designed for laypersons. It usually requires a skilled attorney to navigate the labyrinth of rules to get your case to court.

Also, in addition to knowing the federal rules, you must know the local rules. Every federal district court in America has local rules. These rules are in addition to the Federal Rules of Civil Procedure and they are, if you will, the home spin for that district. You've heard the expression, "well, in Alabama, we do things this way." Well, that's how it works in the federal courts too. The local rules in Alabama may be very different than the local rules in New York.

For example, in Maryland, there is a somewhat unique rule which prohibits any party or lawyer from calling any other party or witness by his or her first name. Obviously, this is the kind of rule that only a lawyer practicing in Maryland would know. Yet, if you were to violate this rule, you'd run the risk of the federal judge forming a bad impression of you.

To prevent this from happening, some federal judges will *insist* that you hire an attorney to represent you. On the one hand, this is for your own good. You certainly don't want to lose your case just because you were unaware of some technical rule that only a lawyer would know. On the other hand, federal judges are extremely concerned about running efficient trials.

Over the past 10 years, Congress has passed a number of federal laws cracking down on violent crime and drug trafficking. As a citizen, that's great news. However, the increase in criminal trials at the federal level has left judges with less time for civil matters. As a result, federal judges must run their civil trials with greater efficiency than ever before. This is only possible when all of the players know the rules.

Therefore, even if you're confident that you can run a smooth trial, the judge may disagree and force you to hire a lawyer. Most often, you will have to do so at your own expense, unless you qualify as "indigent," in which case you could request the court to appoint counsel to represent you in a *pro bono* capacity (free of charge). However, very few federal employees qualify for indigent status. And even then, you probably won't get a court appointed attorney unless the judge thinks that you have a really good chance of winning your case.

Therefore, if you go to federal court, you'll probably have to invest in a good lawyer. And you can expect to pay higher legal fees than you would in an administrative hearing. After all, a jury trial is going to last longer than a hearing before an administrative judge. On the other side of the coin, since the trial process is so much longer than the administrative process, you should be able to space out your legal fees over a longer period of time. In fact, we have had several clients for whom we've arranged monthly payment plans. In this sense, the greater length of the case enabled our clients to better keep up with the costs.

The Summary Judgment Hurdle

In many ways, the federal litigation process is similar to the administrative process. In both processes, the parties conduct discovery. There is also a summary judgment phase in both processes. However, generally speaking, a federal judge is more likely than his or her administrative counterpart to grant the agency's request for summary judgment.

The purpose of the EEO administrative process is to allow as many people as possible to have their day in court. The same thing can't be said for our federal court system. The volume of cases is simply too great. Federal judges must find ways to get cases out of the system and one way of doing so is through summary judgment.

Therefore, if you have a borderline case on liability, you are at a greater risk of having your case thrown out on summary judgment at the federal level than you would be at the administrative level. Obviously, this is an important factor to consider when deciding to file a lawsuit in federal court.

The Settlement Process

Another method that federal judges use to reduce their caseloads is encouraging settlement. In fact, in many jurisdictions, judges either encourage mediation or downright order it. For example, in Maryland, mediation with a federal judge occurs in virtually all cases after the initial pleading stage.

This can actually be a good thing because mediation often affords you a good insight into how the judge will see your case. As a result, by the end of mediation, you should have a pretty clear idea as to whether your case will pass through summary judgment and whether it has jury appeal. Of course, mediation also allows you the opportunity to resolve your case early and forego many of the costs (and headaches) of litigation.

To illustrate, several years ago, we had a case in which Morris Fischer traveled to Asheville, North Carolina for a settlement conference. Upon arriving, Morris spoke with the judge, who couldn't have been nicer. He welcomed Morris to Asheville and poured him some coffee in chambers. The two spoke about the beauty of the Asheville Mountains and mutual acquaintances briefly before getting down to business. They then turned their attention to the case and, after several hours of negotiation, the agency agreed to meet our client's reasonable demands and the case was settled. Our client got the job he was after and some money for his attorney's fees. And best of all, the settlement occurred early in the case, before discovery and depositions, so our client wasn't force to make a large financial investment in the case.

Our experience has been that federal judges like reasonable people, if no other reason than they like getting rid of cases. As a result, if you're more reasonable in your demands than the agency is in their offer to you, a settlement conference may be the way to go. Defense lawyers who must routinely appear in front of the same judge won't want to look like an obstructionist by rejecting what the judge regards as a reasonable settlement.

Chapter 31

Settlement

While much of this book has been focused on equipping you with the tools to win at the hearing and beyond, we don't want to ignore the very real possibility of settling your case with the agency. Remember, much of the EEO process is geared towards settlement and you may find that the agency is more than willing to pursue this avenue. If so, settlement is certainly an option you should consider carefully, as it has many advantages.

The Advantages of Settlement

Settlement Brings Finality (Usually)

First of all, settlement brings a resolution to the issue, allowing you to move on with your career (and your life). If you're currently involved in the process, then you know that it can be time-consuming and physically and emotionally draining. And while fighting for your rights is certainly worth it, it can also be worthwhile to settle your claim under the right conditions. With your claim settled, you can then begin to refocus on the more enjoyable aspects of your professional and social life, as opposed to thinking about depositions, discovery requests and pre-hearing motions, to name just a few.

Unfortunately, settlement doesn't always put an end to discriminatory behavior. In fact, in some cases, it ushers in an era of retaliation on the part of the manager. Some managers and supervisors don't take a charge of discrimination very well. Some will retaliate immediately and others will wait awhile before subjecting the "troublemaker" to retaliation.

Sometimes, the retaliation will be obvious. Other times, it will be more subtle. Yet, either way, a fair number of successful complainants will encounter retaliation for prior EEO activity. We often advise a client after a settlement to "keep your eyes and ears open" and to not hesitate to question actions by those who have knowledge of their EEO activity.

Remember, retaliation is no more acceptable than the underlying discriminatory action. And fortunately, from a legal standpoint, retaliation is often easier to prove. For instance, to prove your case in a discrimination claim, you have to show that you were treated differently from someone outside of your protected class. This isn't the case in retaliation cases. Furthermore, in many cases, you don't have to show that there was a "tangible employment action." Retaliation, in and of itself, is actionable.

Settlement Can Save Your Time and Effort

Second, settlement can save you a lot of time. As we've seen, the entire EEO process can drag on for a year or more. Therefore, even if you're successful, it's going to be a while before you see any tangible results. A year can be a long time to wait, especially if you're waiting to be reinstated, for example. During that year, you're probably going to have to find another way to earn a living. Therefore, a quick settlement that restores your job or provides some other immediate benefit may be better than waiting to receive the "optimum" result some time in the future.

Settlement Is Less Risky

Third, settlement is always less risky than taking your case to a hearing (or to federal court). The truth of the matter is that litigation, of any kind, is never a "sure thing." This is the case even if you have a rock-solid case built upon a mountain of evidence. We've seen this at times in our own practice. We've represented clients on appeal who seem to have done everything right, but for some reason, they lost at the hearing stage. It happens.

Now, we truly believe that if you follow the guidelines set forth in this book, you will improve your chances of victory. However, there are no guarantees that you will be successful. Therefore, if you get a "fair" settlement offer, you will want to give some serious consideration to accepting it, even if you think you *might* do better at the hearing.

Obtaining the "Right" Settlement

For these reasons, we recommend that you keep an open mind towards settlement. That being said, we don't want you to get the impression that you should take just any settlement. The key is that it be the "right" settlement.

We can't give you any magic formula to determine exactly what the right settlement is for you. Every case is different. And more importantly, every person is different. What might be a great settlement in one situation for one person might be a horrendous settlement in another situation for another person. However, when evaluating settlement offers, the two basic factors to consider are: (1) the amount and type(s) of damages; and (2) the likelihood of your success.

Evaluating the Amount and Type(s) of Damages

To evaluate the strength of the offer, compare it to what you could reasonably expect to receive if you won your case "hands down." In other words, if you make a clear and convincing case to a judge who, in the end, sees the facts just as you present them, what could you expect to receive in terms of compensation – your job back, a promotion, back pay, damages, etc.? Does the settlement offer come close to your "perfect" outcome? If so, you should obviously be more likely to settle because you won't be receiving that much more for the aggravation and risk of taking your case to a hearing. Therefore, the better the offer, the more you should consider settling.

Evaluating the Likelihood of Success

Just the opposite logic applies to the likelihood of your success. The more likely you are to succeed, the less you should want to settle, and vice versa. Obviously, if you have a strong case, you should be more willing to forego settlement, unless it's a settlement that you can easily live with. On the other hand, if your case is weak because, let's say, it lacks definitive corroborative evidence to support some aspects of your claim, you should be more willing to accept a less-than-optimal settlement. In this case, you may be better off settling for less than you deserve than fighting for more than you can reasonably expect to get.

Of course, evaluating the strength of the settlement and your likelihood of success aren't simple propositions. For example, how do you determine how much compensation you are likely to receive as a victim of sexual harassment? Likewise, how do you gauge your likelihood of succeeding in a process that you've never been through before? These aren't easy determinations to make.

Therefore, in this case, you may wish to seek out the advice of an employment lawyer who routinely practices in this area of the law. Because this person has had dozens of these kinds of cases (and has read about hundreds more), he or she may be able to better gauge your chances of success and give you a range of possible recoveries. Now, please understand that a lawyer won't be able to give you a definitive answer (and be wary of the one who tries). Yet, he or she should be able to give you a "ballpark" estimate to help put your employer's offer in context.

And realize that you don't have to turn your case over to a lawyer in order to seek his or her advice on the value of a case. You are simply seeking the opinion of an expert. With this advice, you can choose to settle your claim or you can choose to go forward with or without the assistance of a lawyer. It's totally up to you. Nevertheless, seeking expert advice regarding a possible settlement is probably a good move, regardless of what you ultimately decide.

Alternatively, there are a number of good books that even we turn to in order to evaluate the value of a case. The EEOC generally looks to other cases in which similar amounts were awarded, but it really is a non-scientific method. We have included at the end of this book a reading list of publications that we have found helpful in calculating damages, and in particular those that directly address compensatory damages for federal employee EEO cases.

Negotiating a Fair Settlement

Finally, it's important to keep in mind that a settlement is a *negotiated* process. In other words, each settlement is different, depending upon the negotiating power of the parties. Your employer may settle one non-selection case in one manner and an almost identical non-selection case in a totally different manner. In one case, the complainant may receive the promotion, back pay, interest and compensatory damages. In another case, the complainant may not receive a promotion or any compensation, but merely the promise that he or she will be considered for a future position.

In some cases, this discrepancy will result from the fact that one complainant simply had a stronger case. She may have lined up a slew of eye witnesses and had mounds of documentation proving her case. The other complainant may have been simply relying on a "hunch" or "suspicion." Yet, even if all things are equal, negotiating skills often come into play.

Some complainants arrive at better settlements because they know how to negotiate more effectively. Fortunately, this is a skill that can be learned by almost anyone. And while we certainly can't devote the space in this book required to make you an "expert" negotiator, we can share some techniques with you that may improve your odds of reaching a more favorable settlement with your employer.

To illustrate, let's assume that you didn't get a promotion to a grade 13 level and you believe it's due to discrimination. You bring an EEO action at the administrative level. In evaluating any settlement offer, your first task must be calculated what you could expect to receive from the AJ if you win your case.

Back Pay

One component of your potential damages is back pay. You calculate back pay by adding up the time that has passed from the non-selection date until the present. Let's say it's 18 months. You now calculate the difference in pay from the grade 12 level to the grade 13 level. Let's say it's a difference of $4,000 per year. That means full relief, if you won your case, for back pay is $6,000. You also want to add the value of additional benefits you would have received at the grade 13 level for a year and a half (for example, differences in pensions, etc.). Let's say that's another $5,000. Full relief for back pay and benefits is now $11,000.

Compensatory Damages

Next, you want full relief for compensatory damages. There are two components for compensatory damages. First, there are pecuniary (monetary) damages. These are damages for actual medical expenses paid. You are entitled to recover not only your co-payments, but also the portion of your medical expenses paid for by your insurance company, as well as any amount that was discounted by the medical provider to the insurance company. In short, you are entitled to the "fair market value" of the medical treatment, even if you only paid $10 per visit. You are also entitled to future medical expenses. To get a figure for that, you should consult with your doctor and the billing department for his office. In this example, assume that past bills are $5,000 (even if you only paid $300 in out of pocket expenses) and future bills will be $5,000. Full relief for pecuniary damages is $10,000.

You also are entitled to, if you win, full relief for non-pecuniary damages, which are for pain and suffering. This is not easily measured and there are several books we would recommend that provide more guidance on this issue. One book in particular is entitled *Assessing Compensatory Damages Claims in Federal EEO Cases* by Lucinda A. Riley. This book contains a table which matches up various awards with factors AJs look to in determining non-pecuniary damages. These factors include, but are not limited to: (1) length of medical treatment; (2) the kind of medical treatment; (3) whether a psychologist or psychiatrist was involved; (4) the manner in which complainant's family relationships were damaged (e.g., did the stress of the discrimination cause marital problems that resulted in divorce?); and (5) the manner in which friendships and other social relationships were damaged.

There's no magic formula for non-pecuniary damages, but here are some guidelines. Generally speaking, if you didn't seek much medical treatment, don't expect more than $20,000 for non-pecuniary damages. If you had serious medical treatment and your doctor can definitively testify that this treatment was caused by the specific employment situation for which you are bringing an action, we would highly recommend that you consult with an attorney prior to negotiating your claim. You may even want to pay that attorney hourly to assess your case and negotiate a settlement for you. The several thousand dollars you may pay that attorney could easily result in a financial return many times that amount. Now, assume for the purposes of our example that you assess full relief for non-pecuniary damages at $25,000.

Attorney Fees

There is one final component to relief – attorney fees. Add in all monies you've paid an attorney to consult with you on your case, even if you essentially conducted the matter *pro se*. Assume, for this example, attorney fees totaled $2,000.

Your full relief package is $11,000 + $10,000 + $25,000 + $2,000 = $48,000 and the promotion. Certainly, you shouldn't expect to recover more than that figure. The question becomes how much of that figure should you be willing to settle for? The answer depends on the strength of your case. Again, this is where you may want to have an attorney review your case and give you an opinion. You may have wonderful damages, but if ultimately the AJ determines that you weren't more qualified than the selectee, you lose. You get *nothing*.

If you had a crystal ball, you could tell that you had an X% chance of winning. So you could figure out the true value of the case by multiplying the full value of the case by the chance of winning.

In short, if you think you have a strong chance of winning, you're only going to want to settle for a high percentage of $48,000. If you think you don't have a good chance of winning, you should settle for a low percentage of that figure. There's no exact science to this.

In this case, if you truly have (objectively speaking) a strong chance of prevailing, you should strongly consider settling for 75% of $48,000, which comes to $36,000 plus the promotion, or in some circumstances, a priority consideration. For a low chance of prevailing, you should consider settling for around 10-20% of the $48,000, which comes to $4,800 to $9,600, without the promotion.

Starting the Bidding

Of course, your initial settlement demand shouldn't be your bottom line. There are all kinds of books on negotiating and there are indeed great similarities in all negotiating techniques. Whether you're Donald Trump buying a hotel or Joe down the street buying a used car, we would recommend reading some books on this topic.

One thing you want to be sure *not* to do is to ask for $300,000 as your first settlement offer. That's a good way to never get a counteroffer, or to get a bona fide "low-ball" offer. Everyone asks for $300,000 and very, very few get it. In fact, unless there are serious medicals or years of provable, witnessed race hostility or sexual harassment, the EEOC is highly unlikely to award or uphold such an amount. In our research, only two federal employees have received awards of $300,000.00 in the administrative process (not counting jury awards). In one of those cases, the complainant actually died from the agency's discrimination.

Another way to state this is that you shouldn't make your demand ridiculously higher than your bottom line. For instance, if your bottom line was $13,000, strongly consider starting your demand at $25,000 or $30,000, rather than $200,000. Also, don't go to your bottom line in one jump. Go down in intervals. Leave yourself several steps before you're at your bottom line.

Finally, we have one other important guideline. As you're making your demand, you've got to be able to convince agency counsel as to the merits of your case. Expect to go through some calculations with agency counsel as you're negotiating. Nobody is simply going to hand over $13,000 without some reason for it. Explain that several witnesses will testify as to your superior qualifications. Review your medical treatment. You must be able to convince agency counsel that they are getting a bargain at $13,000.

In closing, the art of negotiating is an art onto itself. Yet, basically, you've got to be realistic and take an honest look at your case. There's an old expression that "money talks." This is especially true regarding settlements. Many of our clients settle once we explain to them the risks involved, the true strengths and weaknesses of their case, the money they're putting at risk, either on contingency or through hourly fees, and the benefits of putting the dispute behind them.

As in any law practice, many clients listen and walk away successful. Others don't and aren't as successful. Some reject a low settlement offer and end up winning many times what they rejected. That happened to us in a case recently. The client was about to accept an amount of money right before the hearing decision was to be issued and in fact did accept it, but the agency backed out at the last second and we won the case. Then the agency had to pony up almost ten times that amount to settle later on. You never know. What you must avoid is making decisions with your heart rather than with your head.

Chapter 32

Hiring an Attorney

In this book, we have covered all of the strategies and techniques you will need to fight for your rights. The purpose of this book was to equip you with enough information to go it alone; if you have to. Yet, you should understand that you don't have to go it alone. You can enlist the help of an attorney who concentrates in this area of the law.

Let's face it. Not everyone has the time, inclination or aptitude to take depositions, prepare written interrogatories, do direct and cross examination, make on-the-spot objections in a hearing, or write briefs. Therefore, after reading this book, you may come to the conclusion that you want to fight for your rights, but you'd rather not have to engage in the "hand-to-hand combat" necessary to do so. In that case, you should feel free to consider hiring an attorney to fight on your behalf.

After all, that's what lawyers do - we advocate for other people. And given that it's our job to do so, we develop a proficiency in doing it. It simply comes from practice. Likewise, if you were to handle dozens of different employment matters for different people, you would be just as good at it. Yet, this is likely your first (and hopefully, last) time through the EEO process. As a result, it's unlikely that you're going to be able to represent yourself as well as someone who does this for a living. This factor alone may be enough of a reason to hire an attorney.

Costs of Hiring a Lawyer

Of course, in many cases, the biggest impediment to hiring a lawyer is the cost involved. Legal fees often range in the area of $200-$400 per hour. And unlike personal injury lawyers, most employment lawyers don't take cases on a contingency basis. In other words, they don't usually make arrangements whereby they *only* take a percentage of your ultimate recovery.

There is a good reason why discrimination lawyers don't charge clients in this manner – not all EEO case recoveries are measured in cash. For example, a successful recovery may be reinstatement in your job or a promotion or pay raise. There is simply no way for your lawyer to collect, say, one-third of your promotion from your supervisor. The same is true if your recovery involves enhanced training opportunities or some other non-financial benefit. This is a tremendous bonus for the client as well because, as the lawyer's fee isn't tied to cash recovery, the lawyer can focus his or her efforts on obtaining the "best" (as opposed to highest cash) settlement.

That being said, you can imagine that legal fees can add up pretty quickly. Yet, in some cases, the legal fees pale in comparison to what you have to gain by winning your case. For example, back pay and interest alone can run into the tens (if not hundreds) of thousands of dollars. Likewise, the difference between pay grades can result in substantial sums when factoring in pension benefits. Therefore, in some cases, it may be too expensive *not* to hire a trained professional to fight on your behalf.

Reimbursement of Fees and Expenses

Furthermore, the agency is required to reimburse you for "reasonable" attorney's fees incurred after the filing of your complaint; if you prevail. Under federal law, employees who prevail on claims under Title VII, the Rehabilitation Act or the EPA are presumptively entitled to reimbursement for attorney's fees and costs, unless special circumstances would render reimbursement unjust. Unfortunately, attorney's fees awards are not available to those who file age discrimination claims under the ADEA. Yet, for those filing Title VII, Rehabilitation Act or EPA claims, the prospect of having their attorney's fees paid is welcome.

It's important to remember that, in order to be reimbursed for attorney's fees, you must "prevail" in the case. By "prevail," we mean that you must ultimately receive some benefit from the agency. Obviously, an award of $100,000 in compensatory damages is "prevailing." However, a complainant may prevail without receiving any monetary compensation by, for instance, being reinstated or promoted. Also, if you settle your case, your settlement may include a provision that requires the agency to pay your attorney's fees.

In addition to being reimbursed for your attorney's fees, you may be reimbursed for other costs incurred in making your case as well. These costs include witness fees, transcript costs, printing and copying costs, and expert fees. Therefore, under federal law, you may be able to have many, if not all, of your expenses reimbursed; provided that you prevail in the case.

One more important word on attorney's fees reimbursement. You will only be reimbursed for "reasonable" attorney's fees. AJs have a wide diversity of opinion about the definition of "reasonable" attorney's fees. We know of at least one case where a client believed that anything he did remotely connected to the case was reimbursable. He called his lawyer seventeen times a week, asking practically for hourly updates on his case. He also refused to attend his deposition and refused to provide medical records to his attorneys in a timely fashion, which led to three discovery motions against him for sanctions. Although he prevailed at the hearing and won a modest sum of money, lo and behold the AJ did *not* award him all of his fees because much of the legal work could have been avoided. It's important to remember that the AJ is only going to award reimbursement that is deemed necessary to prosecute the case.

When to Hire a Lawyer

For some complainants, the question is not "if" but "when" to seek out the assistance of a lawyer. Should they call a lawyer as soon as the discriminatory event occurs? Or should they wait until they're assigned a hearing date? The answer to this question varies depending upon the experience and comfort level of the complainant. A simple rule of thumb is that you should call an attorney when you feel that you *need* to.

That being said, it is rarely helpful to hire an attorney the day before your deposition is to be taken. The best time is either right before you file your formal complaint, or right after you receive the ROI. That way, the attorney can help you in the investigation, or in conducting discovery and pre-hearing motions.

If you've read this book and you've internalized many of the concepts, you may not feel that you need the help of an attorney early in the EEO process. For example, the pre-complaint stage is fairly straightforward and, quite frankly, an attorney may not add much to that process, given your knowledge of the EEO system. Besides, federal law doesn't allow reimbursement for attorneys' fees until after the formal complaint has been filed (other than about two hours for pre-complaint investigation), so you may wish to wait until then before starting the meter running on attorney's fees.

Also, just because attorney's fees are reimbursable after filing the formal complaint doesn't mean that you should necessarily hire a lawyer at this point. Remember, the agency will only pay your legal fees if you "prevail." Therefore, you may wish to obtain an attorney after receiving your Acknowledgment Order.

However, the investigative stage <u>is</u> an excellent time to get some practical advice about the strength of your claim and pointers for information to get included in the factual record. You will still be doing all of the actual work but you will be "coached" in a sense by your attorney. For many clients, this is the "test driving period" before turning over the reins to the lawyer.

Picking the "Right" Lawyer for You

Of course, regardless of "when" you choose to hire a lawyer, you must first give some careful thought as to "whom" you choose as your lawyer. At a minimum, we suggest that you choose someone who has experience in this area of law. Just as you wouldn't consult your optometrist about a heart problem, you shouldn't consult your tax lawyer about your discrimination case. This lawyer, no matter how smart, simply doesn't have the practical experience to help you in your case.

Likewise, just because a lawyer is an employment lawyer, doesn't mean that he or she has the experience to take your case. The EEO process is completely unlike the employment dispute process used in many states. As a result, you need someone who is skilled at this particular type of litigation, as opposed to simply a practitioner with a working familiarity with employment law issues. As in most areas of life, experience counts for a lot.

In fact, in our opinion, relevant experience should be right at the top of your list of criteria for choosing an attorney. And don't feel that you have to take the attorney's word for it either. Ask for a list of references and, by all means, call a few people on the list to get their opinions.

When talking with these people, you may want to also get a feel for the lawyer's responsiveness. Does he or she return phone calls or emails in a timely manner? You don't want to have to wait days or weeks to get a simple answer to your question. In fact, in the best of all worlds, you should receive regular updates from your attorney informing you as to the status of your case.

On the flip side of that coin, do not expect instantaneous communication from your attorney, even if you get it sometimes. Although we give out our direct email addresses and cell phone numbers to our clients, it can easily be abused. One client called Mr. Snider, one of our partners, at 8:00 a.m., 10:00 a.m. and at noon, and sent an email at 9:00 a.m. Of course, Mr. Snider was in a hearing from 8-12 so he didn't get any of those calls or the email until the hearing ended. So what did he get when he called the client at 12:30? A grateful 'thanks for calling me back?' Of course not. He got an earful about how he was "out of touch" and "hard to reach."

It isn't very realistic to expect *instantaneous* communication from your attorney. Now in the case of an emergency, your attorney should be available, and if there is more than one attorney in the firm, all of them should have some familiarity with each case – to cover for each other and ensure prompt attention to your needs.

Another important criterion for choosing a lawyer is determining if you have a "personality fit." Now, please understand that we're not suggesting that you and your lawyer have to be best friends. Actually, for a number of reasons, you shouldn't be. On the other hand, you shouldn't hire a lawyer that you can't stand. This is true even if he or she comes highly recommended and is a recognized expert in the field.

As we've discussed several times before, the EEO process can last quite a while and during this rather stressful time, you're going to have to work very closely with your attorney. You certainly don't want to add any additional stress to the situation by teaming up with a person who drives you crazy. Trust us. There's enough craziness in this system as it is. There's no need to add to it.

One other important piece of advice in choosing your lawyer is to beware of one who assures you victory, especially at the initial consultation. No lawyer can make that assurance. At our office, we generally will first review the client's Report of Investigation for a fee. After that review, we meet with the client to review various aspects of the ROI and to give the client an opportunity to explain his or her case to us and address the agency's side of it. We then issue a report giving our assessment of the case.

After all of those steps, if both our office and the client feel comfortable with the case, we'll take it. Over the years of this practice, we have accepted cases and advised complainants not to pursue cases, and we've rejected cases. It's a small investment on the client's part, but even those clients whose cases we didn't take leave with a certain peace of mind that they looked into the matter with a professional and decided that it was best to put it behind them.

Conclusion

In closing, we wish you luck in your pursuit of justice in the workplace. Our purpose in writing this book was to give you the tools necessary to fight for your rights if you are ever the victim of unlawful discrimination. It is our belief that the information contained in this book will do just that.

However, we have not stopped with just writing this book. Each of the sample forms in this book is also available for download at our website at: http://www.sniderlaw.com.

Finally, we want to extend this invitation to contact us should you need assistance in fighting unlawful discrimination. Whether you need someone to fight on your behalf or you just need a seasoned professional to give you an honest assessment of your case, please feel free to contact us at:

Michael J. Snider, Esq.
Snider & Associates, LLC
104 Church Lane, Suite 201
Baltimore, MD 21208
Toll Free: 1-800-DISCRIMINATION
Phone: 410-653-9060
Fax: 410-653-9061
mike@sniderlaw.com
www.sniderlaw.com

Appendix A

Sample Request for a Hearing

U.S. EQUAL EMPLOYMENT OPPORTUNITY COMMISSION
WASHINGTON FIELD OFFICE
1400 L Street, Suite 200
Washington, DC 20005

IN THE MATTER OF:	**Current EEO File No.:**
	EEOC 123-45-6789X
Ive Ben Wronged,	
Complainant,	
vs.	
	AGENCY #1-H-234-4567-89
Daniel Glickman,	
Secretary, Department of Agriculture,	**OFO Appeal #01234567**
Agency.	

MOTION TO CONSOLIDATE CASES
MOTION FOR SANCTIONS
REQUEST FOR A HEARING

Complainant requests that all of her outstanding cases be consolidated for hearing, and that the Agency be Sanctioned for repeated and unjustified failures to process EEO Complaints # 987654, # 654321, #321000 as well as failure to process eleven additional informal EEO complaints dating back many years.

FACTUAL HISTORY

Complainant, Ms. Ive Ben Wronged, has been engaged in a long process against the Agency for numerous EEO actions based primarily upon disability discrimination, failure to accommodate and retaliation. Her complaints commenced September 28, 1995, with the filing of Complaint No. #987654. She later brought two other complaints, #654321, dated April 30, 1996, and #321000, commenced July 23, 1996.

With respect to the first action, that pertained to a breached settlement agreement which was subsequently appealed (see exhibit #1). The Office of Federal Operations ruled that the agency had in fact breached several provisions of the agreement and afforded Complainant the remedy of her complaint's reinstatement.

The second and third actions were eventually consolidated and there were several mediation orders (see exhibit "4"). Upon failure to obtain a settlement, the actions were to be turned back to an Administrative Judge for hearing. Years went by and Complainant heard nothing from the Agency or the EEOC regarding the hearing. Complainant did virtually everything in her power to obtain information regarding the hearing, including having her Congressman, investigate the matter.

In addition to the three formal complaints filed by Complainant, she filed eleven informal complaints. These were pursued by a prior attorney in a letter dated, February 15, 2001. Ms. Wronged was never given to right to file formal complaints with respect to each of these, even though she requested same.

After reviewing complainant's file, by new Counsel, Snider & Associates, LLC., Complainant sought a formal inquiry into the status of the complaints and requested that the agency consent to consolidation of all the matters for a hearing (see exhibit "7"). Such correspondence was sent November 4, 2003 and later follow-up was sent advising of Complainant's intention to bring a motion. No written response was received. In January 2004, Complainant sent a Motion for Sanctions and a Request for a Hearing to the Chief Administrative Law Judge at the EEOC in Washington, DC, which, to date, has not been responded to by Defense Counsel or the Court.

APPLICABLE LAW

29 C.F.R. Section 1614(f) (3) states

> "When the complainant, or the agency against which a complaint is filed, or its employees fail without good cause shown to respond fully and in timely fashion to an order of an administrative judge, or requests for the investigative file, for documents, records, comparative data, statistics, affidavits, or the attendance of witness(es), the administrative judge shall, in appropriate circumstances:
>
> (i) Draw an adverse inference that the requested information, or the testimony of the requested witness, would have reflected unfavorably on the party refusing to provide the requested information;
>
> (ii) Consider the matters to which the requested information or testimony pertains to be established in favor of the opposing party;
>
> (iii) Exclude other evidence offered by the party failing to produce the requested information or witness;

         (iv) Issue a decision fully or partially in favor of the opposing party; or

         (v) Take such other actions as appropriate."

In the case at bar, the least Complainant's counsel should be entitled to is written correspondence from the Agency, acknowledging receipt of its representation and cooperation in setting forth a plan of action to either: (1) consolidate the complaints for a single hearing; (2) providing a detailed account of the status of the informal complaints filed; and (3) provide correct information regarding the status of the latter two formal complaints.

There also exists an issue as to the timeliness of the reinstated complaint with respect to completing a timely investigation. The regulations mandate that the Agency must conduct the investigation within 180 days of the complaint's filing. The agency is also required to develop complete and factual records upon which to make findings in on the matters raised by the written complaint. Thus far, the only Agency communication acknowledging its duty to investigate her is the aforementioned August 2003 letter, describing a previous letter with Complainant on August 8, 2003, indicating that her complaint had been reinstated. However, there was considerable time, years that went by, in which no investigation had been completed. Instead, the Agency hid behind an allegation that Complainant had held up the process through her failure to return the $99,000.00 compensatory damage award, which she never accepted.

While the Agency may argue that the 180 day requirement has not passed, by virtue of its August Correspondence, Counsel for Complainant would have no way of knowing what, if any, investigation was performed or if the Agency was planning on completing one, due to its lack of response to Complainant's simple request for acknowledgement. Motions such as this only become necessary due to this lack of cooperation.

Finally, given that Complainant's actions have dragged on for some eight to nine years, it is unfair to her to further wait for an Agency response. Instead, Counsel respectfully requests that the Chief Administrative Law Judge investigate this matter in order to get the complaints processed, hearings scheduled and arrange for possible consolidation.

_____

Michael J. Snider, Esq.
Snider & Associates, LLC
104 Church Lane, Suite 201
Baltimore, MD 21208
410-653-9060 voice
410-653-9061 fax

Appendix B

Sample Interrogatories

EQUAL EMPLOYMENT OPPORTUNITY COMMISSION
BALTIMORE FIELD OFFICE
10 South Howard Street
Baltimore, MD 21201

Jane Doe,	)	
	)	
COMPLAINANT,	)	**EEOC NO. XXX-XXXX-XXXXXX**
	)	
vs.	)	
	)	**AGENCY CASE NO.: XXXXX**
Department of Defense,	)	
Defense Contact Audit Agency	)	
	)	
AGENCY.	)	
	)	

COMPLAINANT'S INTERROGATORIES

Complainant, through her counsel, Snider and Fischer LLC, requests that the Agency respond to the following interrogatories. You are required to answer these interrogatories separately and fully in writing, under oath. You are required to respond to these interrogatories no later than thirty (30) calendar days after receipt of these interrogatories, to the undersigned at 104 Church Lane Suite 201, Baltimore, Maryland 21208.

INSTRUCTIONS

A.   Each Interrogatory is to be answered fully on the basis of information which is in your possession.

B.   In each of your answers to these Interrogatories, you are requested to provide not only such information as is in your possession, but also information as is reasonably available. In the event that you are able to provide only part of the information called for by any particular Interrogatory, please provide all the information you are able to provide and state the reason for your inability to provide the remainder.

C.   If you object to or otherwise decline to answer any portion of an Interrogatory, please provide all information called for by that portion of the Interrogatory to which you do not object or to which you do not decline to answer. For those portions of an Interrogatory to which you object or to which you do not decline to answer, state the reason for such objection or declination.

D.   Every Interrogatory herein shall be deemed a continuing interrogatory and information in addition to or in any way inconsistent with your initial answer to such Interrogatory.

E.   If any of the following Interrogatories can be answered fully and completely simply by referring to an exhibit number, page, and paragraph of the investigative file compiled by the Agency and furnished to the Complainant by the Agency in connection with this administrative complaint of discrimination, such references, if adequately identified to inform the Complainant as to your response will serve as a satisfactory response to such Interrogatory.

DEFINITIONS

A.   "Complainant" means Jane Doe.

B.   "Agency," "you," "your," or "yourself," means the Department of Defense, Defense Contact Audit Agency, the named Agency in this case, and any and all of its agents, representatives, employees, servants, consultants, contractors, subcontractors, investigators, attorneys, and any other persons or entities acting or purporting to act on behalf of the agency.

C.   "Person", "persons," "people", and "individual" means any natural person, together with all federal, state, county, municipal and other government units, agencies or public bodies, as well as firms, companies, corporations, partnerships, proprietorships, joint ventures, organizations, groups of natural persons or other associations or entities separately identifiable whether or not such associations or entities have a separate legal existence in their own right.

D.   "Document," "documents," and "writing" means all records, papers, and books, transcriptions, pictures, drawings or diagrams or every nature, whether transcribed by hand or by some mechanical, electronic, photographic or other means, as well as sound reproductions of oral statements or conversations by whatever means made, whether in your actual or constructive possession or under your control or not, relating to or pertaining to or in any way to the subject matters in connection which it is used and includes originals, all file copies, all other copies, no matter how prepared and all drafts prepared in connection with such writing, whether used or not, including by way of illustration and not by way of limitation, the following; books; records; reports; contracts; agreements; expense accounts; canceled checks; catalogues; price lists; video, audio and other electronic recordings; memoranda (including written memoranda of telephone conversations, other conversations, discussions, agreements, acts and activities); minutes; diaries; calendars; desk pads; scrapbooks; notes; notebooks; correspondence; drafts; bulletins; electronic mail; facsimiles; circulars; forms; pamphlets; notice; statements; journals; postcards;

letters; telegrams; publications; inter- and intra- office communications; photostats; photographs; microfilm; maps; drawings; diagrams; sketches; analyses; electromagnetic records; transcripts; and any other documents within defendant's possession, custody or control from which information can be obtained or translated, if necessary, by detection devices into reasonably usable form, i.e. typed in English prose.

E.   "Communication" or "communications" means any and all inquiries, discussions, conferences, conversations, negotiations, agreements, meetings, interviews, telephone conversations, letters correspondence, notes telegrams, facsimiles, electronic mail, memoranda, or other forms of communications, including but not limited to both oral and written communications.

F.   "Produce" and "provide" mean to provide either a legible true copy of the original or any document and/or communication.

G.   "Relate to," "relating to," "concerning," "pertain," and "pertaining to," mean consisting of, referring to, reflecting or arising out of, evidencing or in any way legally, logically, or factually connected with the matter discussed, directly or indirectly.

H.   "Identify," "identifying," and "identification" when referring to a person mean to provide an identification sufficient t notice a deposition of such person and to serve such person with process to require his or her attendance at a place of examination and shall include, without limitation, his or her full name, present or last known address, present or last known business affiliation, home and business telephone number, title or occupation, each of his or her positions during the applicable period of time covered by any answer referring to such person and relationship, if any, to the agency.

I.   "Identify," "identifying," and "identification" when used in reference to a writing or document mean to give a sufficient characterization of such writing or document to properly identify it in a request to produce and shall include, without limitation, the following information with respect to teach such document:

  1.   The date appearing on such document, and if it has no date, the answer shall so state and shall give the date or approximate date such document was prepared;

  2.   The identity or descriptive code number, file number, title or label of such document;

  3.   The general nature and description of such document, and if it was not signed, the answer shall so state and shall give the name of the person or persons who prepared it;

  4.   The names of the person(s) to whom such docum1ent was addressed and the name of each person other than such addressee to whom such document or copies of it, were given or sent;

5.   The name(s) of the person(s) having present possession, custody, or control of such document(s); and

6.   Whether or not any draft, copy or reproduction of such document contains any postscripts, notations, changes or addendum not appearing on the document itself, and if so, the answer shall give the description of each such draft, copy or reproduction.

J.   Subject position – Subject position is the position known as DCAA (JOA) #NE 2002-0030 covering GS-511-13 Supervisory Auditor Position.

In answering these interrogatories, the agency is requested to furnish not only such information as is available to the agency but also such information as is known to any of the agency's agents, representatives, employees, servants, consultants, contractors, subcontractors, investigators, attorneys, and any other person or entity acting or purporting to act on behalf of the agency.

In any matter responsive to any of the interrogatories the agency shall set forth completely the grounds for the asserted privilege, along with copies of the Privacy Act provisions or other written materials upon which such assertion is made. The agency shall identify as to each privileged communication or document:

1.   its date;

2.   its author(s);

3.   the business title or position of its author(s);

4.   its recipient(s);

5.   the business title or position of its recipient(s);

6.   its number of pages;

7.   its stated subject matter;

8.   the legal basis upon which the agency claims privilege;

9.   the specific portion of the interrogatory or document to which the communication or document is responsive.

Documents are to be labeled to indicate the interrogatory to which they respond. In order to simplify the issues and resolve as many matters of fact as possible before hearing, if, following a reasonable and thorough investigation using due diligence, you are unable to answer any interrogatory, or any part thereof, in full, because sufficient information is not available to you, answer the interrogatory to the maximum extent possible, including any knowledge or belief you have concerning the unanswered portion thereof and the facts upon which such knowledge or belief is based. In addition, state what you did to locate the missing information and why that information is not available to you.

When an exact answer to an interrogatory is not known, state the best estimate available, state that it is an estimate, and state the basis for such estimate.

If documents once in your possession or under your control are requested or are the subject of an interrogatory, and such documents are no longer in your possession or under your control, state when such documents were must recently in your possession or under your control, and what disposition was made of them, including identification of the person now in possession of or exercising control over such documents. If the documents were destroyed, state when and where they were destroyed, and identify the person or persons who directed their destruction.

All of the following interrogatories shall be continuing in nature until the date of the hearing, and you must supplement your answers as additional information becomes known or available to you.

NOTE

IF ANY INTERROGATORY OR REQUEST IS OBJECTIONABLE, PLEASE CALL COUNSEL FOR THE COMPLAINANT BEFORE OBJECTING, IN ORDER TO ATTEMPT TO NARROW THE QUESTION OR AVOID THE OBJECTIONABLE PORTION OR ASPECT.

IDENTIFY ALL DOCUMENTS ASSOCIATED WITH EACH INTERROGATORY.

COMPLAINANT'S INTERROGATORIES

1. Identify all persons answering or supplying information used in answering these Interrogatories.

2. State the name, address, and business telephone number of each person with personal knowledge regarding the facts and circumstances surrounding the happenings of the occurrences referred to in the complaint.

3. State and describe in detail all evidence including documents, affidavits and/or statements not in the Report of Investigation upon which you intend to rely, or submit at the hearing.

4. Identify all individuals who had input into the decision to post the subject position and to select the Selectee, _____.

5. Describe the selection process in step by step detail as to how candidates were evaluated and selected for the subject position.

6. Explain fully the safeguards used, if any, employed and put into place by the Selecting and/or recommending officials and communicated to the supervisors/managers involved in the candidate selection for the purpose to protect against possible or potential bias or discriminatory actions prohibited by law in the selection process.

7.   Identify and explain the stated criteria given by the Selecting Official and/or selection panel, either individually or jointly, or by and through the coordinating Selecting Official, to be used in selecting a candidate for the subject position.

8.   Explain any changes that occurred within the last five years to the duties and responsibilities of the subject position and how those changes affected the selection process.

9.   List in detail all reasons that the selectee, _____, was selected for the subject position.

10.   List in detail all reason that Jane Doe was not selected.

11.   List all information relied upon by all the managers and the selecting officials in selecting the selectee for the position in question.

12.   Please list all information relied upon by all the managers and selecting officials to not select the Complainant for the position in question.

13.   Explain why no interviews were given to any of the candidates.

14.   Were all OPM and agency policies, rules and procedures in the selection process followed? If not, please state: (a) each policy, rule or procedure not followed; (b) the individual failing to follow the rule, procedure or policy; and (c) the reason for the rule, procedure or policy having been violated.

15.   Under what legal authority (rule, procedure or policy) was the disallowance of 15 points from complainant's rating relied upon.

16.   Identify all corporate cost audits that the Selectee performed and their locations upon which the Agency considered in his promotion to this position.

17.   Was _____ aware that the Selectee had a statement of limited mobility in his career profile prior to recommending him for the position?

18.   Was _____ aware that the Selectee had on file a statement of limited mobility when he selected him?

19.   Did anyone from the agency speak with the Selectee prior to or following his selection regarding his limited mobility designation statement? If yes, identify: (a) the individual who spoke with Strong; (b) the date of such conversation; and (c) the sum and substance of the conversation.

20.   Within the previous 5 years, identify all employees under the direct supervision (one step of command only) of _____. State the individual's name, gender, title and grade level.

21. Within the previous 5 years, identify all promotions or hirings to which _____ or _____ were either a recommending official, selecting official or had input into the decision. For each promotion or hire state: (a) the nature of the aforesaid employment decision; (b) whether _____ or _____ had the aforesaid input; (c) the names and genders of each competing candidate to which either _____ or _____ had an opportunity to recommend, select or have input into the decision some other way; (d) the nature of the input given and; (e) the name and gender of each candidate either recommended or selected.

22. List all charges, investigations and complaints of discrimination due to gender, race or age filed in the last ten years against anyone who had input in the final decision of who to promote to the subject position.

Respectfully Submitted,

Date:_____

_____
Morris E. Fischer , Esq.
Attorney for Complainant

Appendix C

Sample Request for Admissions

COMPLAINANT'S REQUESTS FOR ADMISSIONS

Complainant, through his attorney, Michael J. Snider, Esq., requests that you admit to the following facts pursuant. If you deny any one of the following, you are to state with particularity the basis for said denial and to attach to your denial supporting documentation. You are required to fully respond to these Requests no later than twenty (20) calendar days after receipt of these interrogatories, to the undersigned . The Instructions and Definitions found in Complainant's Interrogatories apply here.

REQUESTS FOR ADMISSIONS

1. On September 22, 2002, you reassigned Mr. Client to your office to work directly for you.

2. You did not notify Mr. Client that you had reassigned him.

3. You did not provide a copy of the SF-50 reassignment action to Mr. Client.

4. In response to his request dated December 11, 2002, for a copy of his current position description (PD), you provided a copy of PD #_____ to Mr. Client as an enclosure to your letter dated December 19, 2002.

5. PD#_____ is not current.

6. PD #_____ is not accurate.

7. PD #_____ describes a position with the obsolete title of _____ assigned in the _____.

8. You abolished the position of _____ assigned in the _____ in a recent reorganization.

9.   PD #_____ states, under the factor of Supervisory controls, that the incumbent reports to the _____.

10.   PD# _____ is misclassified as to title.

11.   PD #_____ is misclassified as to grade level.

12.   There is no evaluation report attached to the PD.

13.   Assignment of Mr. Client to a position/PD known to be misclassified and overgraded deprived him of his RIF placement rights to a continuing GS-15 position.

14.   You held a "Town Hall Meeting" in December, _____ of all employees.

15.   At that meeting, you introduced Mr. Client as the designated _____.

16.   At that meeting, you told the staff, publicly, that upon his return from his _____ assignment, Mr. Client would be officially assuming the duties of the position of designated _____.

17.   Present at that "Town Hall Meeting" were the following employees:

18.   This list is representative of those employees in attendance, but is not all inclusive.

19.   Following the Town Hall Meeting, you asked Mr. Client to meet with his assigned staff.

20.   Mr. Client did meet with his assigned staff.

21.   In the capacity of Acting _____, Mr. Client conferred on several other occasions in person, via e-mail and by telephone with his assigned staff on current issues and program plans.

22.   In mid-March, 2002, when Mr. Client informed you by telephone and e-mail of his pending return on June 1, 2002, you did not tell him that you had decided to permanently promote X into the position of Director..

23.   The position you permanently promoted X into was the very same position that you had announced publicly that Mr. Client would be returning to in the December 2000 Town hall Meeting.

24.   By publicly announcing his reassignment to the _____ position you made it clear that Mr. Client did not need to compete for the temporary promotion to that position.

25.   You did not afford Mr. Client an opportunity to compete for that position.

26.   You did not inform Mr. Client that the position was posted for competition.

27.   You did not inform Mr. Client in advance of your decision to promote X permanently into the position that you had promised to Mr. Client.

28.   Restriction of competition constitutes a prohibited personnel practice.

29.   You asked Mr. Client to develop the PD for _____.

30.   Mr. Client submitted to you the PD for _____ on July 9, 2002.

31.   You have not graded the PD for _____.

32.   You have not classified the PD for _____.

33.   You have not reassigned Mr. Client into the PD for _____.

34.   You have not detailed Mr. Client into the PD for _____.

35.   You have not provided any official paperwork (e.g., form SF-50, etc.) to Mr. Client to show that Mr. Client was returned to a GS-Y continuing position at _____ in June, 2002, following his _____.

36.   You have not provided Mr. Client with any official documentation for the "detail" you claim he is on to your office since June 1, 2002.

37.   You have not provided Mr. Client with performance standards for that detail since June 1, 2002.

38.   You have not provided Mr. Client with performance standards for his permanent position of record, since June 1, 2002.

39.   You have not provided Mr. Client with a performance appraisal since June 2000.

40.   A submitted to you interim performance appraisals for the period June 2000-June 2002.

41.   A submitted to you final performance appraisals for the period June 2000-June 2002.

42.   You did not provide Mr. Client a copy of the interim performance appraisals submitted to you by A

43.   You did not provide Mr. Client a copy of the final performance appraisals submitted to you by A

44.   You have not considered Mr. Client for awards or bonuses based on his performance appraisals.

45. Mr. Client returned to duty from his 2 year assignment with Z on June 1, 2002.

46. Since June 1, 2002, you have not taken any action to reassign Mr. Client to the position of T which you had him develop in July 2002.

47. Mr. Client has never refused to complete any work assignment.

48. Mr. Client has completed all work assignments you have given him in an exemplary manner.

49. Mr. Client has completed all work assignments you have given him within the policy guidelines and timeframes assigned.

50. Mr. Client volunteered in Fall 2002 to take responsibility for completing the classification review of all G positions.

51. Mr. Client volunteered to, and did in fact, develop within two weeks new PDs and evaluation reports for G positions in grades GS-5 through GS-11.

52. Mr. Client volunteered to take on additional work in an E-mail to you dated October 15, 2002.

53. Mr. Client submitted medical documentation in support of his request for sick leave to you on November 12, 2002, following his office visit that same day with Dr. _____.

54. You waited fourteen (14) calendar days, until 3:00 PM on November 27, 2002, to inform Mr. Client by telephone of your intention to charge him with AWOL for the entire leave period from November 18, 2002, through November 29, 2002, the leave period supported by the medical certificate he submitted to you on November 12, 2002.

55. Mr. Client submitted another medical certificate from Dr. _____ to you on November 27, 2002, prior to close of business, in support of his sick leave request for the pay period November 18 through November 29, 2002.

56. You did not address the additional medical information in Mr. Client's November 27, 2002, medical certificate in your refusal to grant his sick leave request.

57. You have not spoken with or corresponded with Dr. _____ regarding his medical evaluation of Mr. Client.

58. You could have sent Mr. Client to an Agency physician for an examination.

59. You have not sent Mr. Client to an Agency physician for an examination.

60. In your e-mail letter to Mr. Client dated August 14, 2002, you stated in regard to his

assignment to develop an accountability program/system for the department that he had submitted a voluminous amount of work that you did not have time to review.

61.   You stated in the 8/14/02 email that you had no more accountability work to assign him at that time.

62.   You stated in the 8/14/02 email that you were placing him on sick leave.

63.   Mr. Client had not requested sick leave for that period of time.

64.   Your placing him on sick leave was an unannounced furlough.

65.   You kept Mr. Client in involuntary sick leave status, against his will, for 7 consecutive workdays.

66.   Placement of an employee in AWOL or other involuntary leave for more than 14 consecutive days constitutes a "constructive suspension."

67.   Mr. Client has and routinely makes use of a state-of-the art 2.2 GHZ computer with DVD and CD burners and a 120GB hard drive, an 18" LCD monitor, a laser jet printer, a scanner, a videoconferencing camera, two inkjet printers, a Fax machine, a teleconferencing speakerphone, an intercom, and/or special halogen and other lighting in his home office.

68.   Allowing Mr. Client to work at home would not have presented an "undue hardship" to the Agency.

69.   Mr. Client requested the name, title and address of a VA Orthopedic Surgeon who specializes in foot and ankle surgery from Ms. _____.

70.   Mr. Client requested the name, title and address of a VA Orthopedic Surgeon who specializes in foot and ankle surgery from Ms. _____ so that he could provide to that person the medical documentation requested in _____'s letter of December 4, 2002.

71.   Ms. _____ never provided Mr. Client the name, title and address of a VA Orthopedic Surgeon who specializes in foot and ankle surgery.

72.   You provided reasonable accommodation for Mr. Client to work at home from July 5, 2002, through October 25, 2002.

73.   This reasonable accommodation was for Mr. Client's physical disability.

74.   This reasonable accommodation presented no "undue hardship" to the Agency.

75.   This reasonable accommodation was effective.

76.   The Agency has a Telework program in effect.

77.   The Telework program was in effect at least since January 2002.

78.   Telework is a form of flexiplace.

79.   One form of telework is work at home.

80.   Work at home is a form of reasonable accommodation under the ADA.

81.   Telework is not limited to any particular occupations and/or grade levels.

82.   "Virtual Staff" are employees who work at home.

83.   Virtual Staff utilize the Telework program for their entire tour of duty.

84.   The Agency employs Virtual Staff.

85.   There are cost savings associated with the employment of "virtual staff."

86.   You are currently recruiting for additional "virtual employees?"

87.   You served on an interagency panel on telework.

Respectfully Submitted,

_____
Michael J. Snider, Esq.
Attorney for Complainant

Appendix D

Sample Discovery Objections

EQUAL EMPLOYMENT OPPORTUNITY COMMISSION
BALTIMORE DISTRICT OFFICE

IN THE MATTER OF:	]	**Current EEO File No.:**
	]	EEOC 123-45-6789X
Ive Ben Wronged,	]	
	]	
Complainant,	]	
	]	
vs.	]	
	]	AGENCY #1-H-234-4567-89
Secretary, Department of the Navy,	]	OFO Appeal #01234567
	]	
Agency.	]	

COMPLAINANT'S OBJECTIONS AND RESPONSES TO AGENCY'S INTERROGATORIES

GENERAL OBJECTIONS: Complainant hereby OBJECTS to the Agency's Discovery on the grounds that said Discovery is overbroad, vague, overly burdensome, requests irrelevant, immaterial or inadmissible information or information protected by privilege, and/or contains multipart questions in violation of law, rule or regulation.

Interrogatory No. 1: Please provide the name, location, address, and telephone numbers of any and all witnesses who will testify in person and/or via affidavit or deposition on your behalf at the EEOC hearing.

OBJECTIONS: Complainant reiterates his General Objections and adds that he has not determined yet which witnesses "who will testify" and therefore this Interrogatory is premature. The following individuals **may** testify and/or have relevant information.

RESPONSE: Complainant contends that the following persons will be called to testify in person and/or via affidavit or deposition:

Arnold Sweater
Dana Sweater
Rabbi Hillel Teeshirt
Dr. Robert Blouse
Ronald Cufflink
Keith Ringaround
David Buttonhole

Interrogatory No. 2: State the relationship of each witness identified in Interrogatory No. 1 to your case and how long you have known each witness.

OBJECTIONS: Relevance.

RESPONSE: Complainant contends that the following relationships to the Complainant are held for persons identified in Interrogatory No. 1:

Name	Relationship	Known for how long
Arnold Sweater	Self	N/A
Dana Sweater	Spouse	15 yrs
Rabbi Hillel Teeshirt	Jewish Orthodox Rabbi	12 yrs
Dr. Robert Blouse	Treating physician/psychiatrist	3 years
Ronald Cufflink	Colleague	20 yrs
Keith Ringaround	Colleague	22 yrs
David Buttonhole	Colleague	21 yrs

Interrogatory No. 3: Provide a summary of the expected testimony of each witness identified in response to Interrogatory No. 1.

OBJECTIONS: Complainant reiterates and restates each Objection from above, and adds that this Interrogatory requests information subject to privilege, including attorney work product. Without waiving any privilege, Complainant responds as follows:

RESPONSE: Complainant contends that the following is a summary of the expected testimony for persons identified in Interrogatory No. 1:

Name	Summary of testimony
Arnold Sweater	ABC and DE Division management officials have created a hostile workplace environment and have treated the Complainant adversely because of his religion and have retaliated against him because of his prior EEO activity and EEO related complaints. Complaints include but are not limited to being treated differently with respect to the terms and conditions of the Complainant's

employment, lower than deserved performance ratings, restrictions on collaborations, slower than normal purchase request approvals, more stringent work monitoring than applied to others, and imposed work monitoring that is not mandated by the Complainant's job description.

Official requests for an adjusted work schedule to accommodate the Complainant's religious observances and family responsibilities due to the disabling and chronic health condition of my spouse have not been approved even though they would cause no undue hardship to the Agency.

On a continuous basis the Complainant has been denied reassignment to a more productive work environment where hostility and discrimination do not exist.

On a continuous basis management officials have diminished and denigrated the Complainant's accomplishments and those of other Jews (or those perceived to be Jewish) currently or formerly in the ABCDE Division.

The ABCDE Division has an ongoing pattern and practice of anti-Semitism and prejudice.

On a continuous basis the Complainant has made his concerns known to Division management officials, the IG Office, and EEO Office, about discrimination and hostile work place environment. However, management officials have been non-responsive and have failed to act to correct the situation. The work place has contributed to increased distress, frustration, impatience, anxiety, sleeplessness, strained family relations, and a decrease in enjoyment of life (i.e., a depressed outlook) for the Complainant. The Complainant is tired and frustrated with the discrimination at work. The Complainant has decreased energy, impatience, and is drained from dealing with poor managers and too few supportive colleagues at work. The Complainant often desires to quit work due to unfair ratings and reviews, continuous nit-picking and trivial fault-finding. Other examples of discrimination at work are badgering of the Complainant and held up manuscripts. Examples of damages this has caused the Complainant at home are difficult relationships with his wife and children, etc.

The Complainant is a loyal, dedicated, and trustworthy Navy employee.

Dana Sweater	On a continuous basis the Complainant worries about his livelihood because of discrimination and a hostile work place environment. Work related problems have contributed to adverse emotional and physical health effects, e.g., increased distress, frustration, impatience, anxiety, sleeplessness, and a decrease in the Complainant's enjoyment of life (i.e., a depressed outlook). Difficult relationships at home (with wife and children) have resulted from the discrimination and mistreatment of the Complainant at work. The Complainant is a hardworking, caring, and dedicated husband and father.
Rabbi Hillel Teeshirt	The Complainant has daily religious and moral obligations, to include conducting morning and afternoon prayers, caring for wife and family, earning a livelihood, giving to charitable organizations, etc. The Complainant has frequently voiced his concerns about discrimination and a hostile work place environment for himself and other Jewish employees. The Complainant is a loyal, dedicated, and trustworthy Jew.
Dr. Robert Blouse	The Complainant has voiced concerns about discrimination and a hostile work place environment for many years. The Complainant has raised concerns about his increased distress, frustration, impatience, anxiety, sleeplessness, strained family relations, and a decrease in enjoyment of life (i.e., a depressed outlook). The Complainant has been concerned about having decreased energy, impatience, and difficult relationships with his wife and children.
Ronald Cufflink	The Complainant's scientific research for the Navy is very good. In the Navy organization there are good managers and poor managers. No Jews, good scientific women, or Blacks were put in management positions. Jewish scientists were not promoted despite greater numbers of publications. Another Jewish employee in the Division has also experienced vicious anti-Semitic attacks and a hostile work environment in the Division.
Keith Ringaround	There are cultural problems, a culture of anti-Semitism in the Division, wherein employees and managers shun people and allege the Jews or those perceived to be Jewish are not up to snuff. The Complainant has voiced concerns about discrimination and a hostile work place environment for many years. The Complainant has had undue hardships from his supervisors in publishing, collaborating with other top scientists of his choice, obtaining an approved alternate work schedule, spending customer funds that he brought in to the Laboratory, obtaining advanced leave for Jewish

	holidays, obtaining fair performance ratings based on merit and achievement, and obtaining a transfer to a more productive research group where no discrimination or prejudice exists. The Complainant is a loyal, dedicated, and trustworthy Navy employee.
David Buttonhole	The ABCDE Division has an ongoing pattern and practice of anti-Semitism and prejudice. The Complainant has voiced concerns about discrimination and a hostile work place environment for many years. The Complainant has had undue hardships from his supervisors in awarding his last promotion, publishing manuscripts, collaborating with other Jewish scientists, obtaining an approved alternate work schedule, borrowing leave for Jewish holidays, obtaining fair performance ratings based on merit and achievement, and obtaining a transfer to a more productive research group where no discrimination or prejudice exists. Division employees and managers have been overheard to make virulent anti-Semitic remarks and have brought false allegations against Jews and those perceived to be Jewish regarding the value of their research work and productivity. The Complainant is a loyal, dedicated, and trustworthy Navy employee.

Interrogatory No. 4: State the name, location, address, and telephone number of any and all persons who have information that is relevant to the issues in this appeal, but who are not listed in the response to Interrogatory No. 1, and the nature of the information that each of those persons possesses.

OBJECTIONS: Complainant reiterates and restates each Objection from above, and adds that this Interrogatory requests information subject to privilege, including attorney work product, and calls for speculation – i.e., how can Complainant know "all persons who have information that is relevant?" Complainant therefore reserves his right to object to this Interrogatory, and to supplement it with further information.. Without waiving any privilege, Complainant responds as follows:

RESPONSE: Complainant contends that one additional person has information that is relevant to the issues in this case:

Mickey Mouse
Naval Base Toronto, CA

Summary of relevant information: The Complainant and his colleagues have voiced concerns about discrimination and a hostile work place in ABCDE Division for many years. The Complainant is a hard-working, loyal, dedicated, and trustworthy Navy employee. The

Complainant has had undue hardships from his supervisors in publishing, collaborating with other top scientists of his choice, and obtaining a transfer to a more productive research group where no discrimination or prejudice exists.

Interrogatory No. 5: Identify each agency employee you believe committed an act of discrimination, reprisal or other prohibited personnel action against you from January 1, 2000 to December 31, 2004.

OBJECTIONS: Complainant reiterates and restates each Objection from above, and adds that this Interrogatory requests information subject to privilege, including attorney work product. Further, the incidents are so numerous that it is impossible to name them all; the main ones are related here, but Complainant reserves the right to supplement this (and every other) Response. Without waiving any privilege, Complainant responds as follows:

RESPONSE: Complainant contends that the following Agency employees and managers have committed acts of discrimination, reprisal, and prohibited personnel action against the Complainant from January 1, 2000 to December 31, 2004:

1. Mickey Mouse
2. Donald Duck
3. Goofy

Interrogatory No. 6: Describe the precise manner in which you allege each agency employee identified in Interrogatory No. 5 committed a discriminatory act, reprisal or otherwise engaged in a prohibited personnel practice.

OBJECTIONS: Complainant reiterates and restates each Objection from above, and adds that this Interrogatory requests information subject to privilege, including attorney work product. Without waiving any privilege or objection, Complainant responds as follows:

RESPONSE: Complainant contends that the following actions (or inactions) by Agency employees and managers constituted acts of discrimination, reprisal, and prohibited personnel practice against the Complainant:

1. Mickey Mouse
   a. Selected Jon Whitewash in 2001 as Division Chief after the Complainant and others had filed EEO grievances and related complaints against them due to discrimination, anti-Semitism, and/or harassment.
   b. Selected Doug Nazi-in-disguise in 2003 as Division Chief after the Complainant and others had filed EEO grievances and related complaints against them due to discrimination, anti-Semitism, and/or harassment.

2.   Daffy Duck
   a.   As the EEO Office Chief, approved for the Director the appointment of Jon Whitewash in 2001 as Division Chief after the Complainant and others had EEO and related complaints against them due to discrimination, anti-Semitism, and/or harassment.
   b.   As the EEO Office Chief, approved for the Director the appointment of Doug Nazi-in-disguise in 2003 as Division Chief after the Complainant and others had EEO and related complaints against them due to discrimination, anti-Semitism, and/or harassment.

3.   Doug Goofy
   a.   Assigned bogus research objectives to the Complainant with the help of Dennis the Menace, Jon Whitewash, and Ronald McDonald.
   b.   Repeatedly made false allegations against the Complainant regarding the value and quality of the Complainants research and productivity.
   c.   Explanations and proof of the Complainant's achievements were overruled, dismissed or ignored, and were forever subject to nit-picking and trivial fault-finding. The Complainant's supervisors regularly expressed doubts over the Complainant's performance and standard of work, however, the doubts lacked substantive and quantifiable evidence.
   d.   Never offered the Complainant the opportunity to earn religious comp time.
   e.   Repeatedly, rated the Complainant lower than deserved or recommended by other management officials.
   f.   Failed to respond to the Complainant's e-mails about concerns of hostile work place and discrimination from the Complainant's Branch supervisor and Team Leader.
   g.   Previously made the anti-Semitic comment, "The Navy doesn't care if it has Nazis working for it."
   h.   Previously, promoted to high level Division management a vocal Holocaust denier.
   i.   Repeatedly harassed and discriminated against the Complainant's Jewish or Jewish sympathizer colleagues.
   j.   Enabled and fostered a hostile work environment in the Division for Jewish employees and those perceived to be Jewish by failing to take any substantive corrective actions with regard to numerous and repeated complaints by the Complainant and his colleagues about anti-Semitism and discrimination and harassment.

Interrogatory No. 7:   Describe how each act of discrimination, reprisal and/or prohibited personnel practice adversely affected a term or condition of your employment.

OBJECTIONS: Complainant reiterates and restates each Objection from above, and adds that this Interrogatory requests information subject to privilege, including attorney work product. Further, the incidents are so numerous that it is impossible to name them all; the main ones are related here, but Complainant reserves the right to supplement this (and every other) Response. Further, Complainant alleges that this Interrogatory is in part irrelevant, since reprisal claims do not have to prove a tangible employment action. Without waiving any privilege, Complainant responds as follows:

RESPONSE: Complainant contends that the following statements describe how the acts of discrimination, reprisal, and prohibited personnel action given in Interrogatory No. 6 adversely affected the term or conditions of the Complainant's employment:

1. Lower than deserved performance ratings
2. Lower pay increases and/or bonus payouts
3. Delay in publishing
4. Degraded communication and information exchange with other scientists
5. Lower morale and esprit de corps
6. Personal depressed outlook and undue stress
7. Additional EEO grievances, attorney's costs and fees
8. Additional use of leave hours
9. Expenditure of additional effort and time to maintain or increase scientific productivity
10. More stringent work monitoring than applied to others
11. Increased ostracization from Team, Branch, and Division activities
12. Endured harmful reprisals and retaliations
13. Personal agenda and political ambition of managers resulted in continued harassment and discriminatory behaviors encountered by the Complainant and his colleagues.
14. Attempts to impose research requirements and procedures not mandated by the Complainant's job description.
15. Loss of faith in management; managers showed a poor example of Navy leadership.
16. Anti-Semitic slurs and personal support for Holocaust deniers created a hostile work environment for the Jewish Complainant
17. The work and scientific ethics of managers were sub-standard.
18. Managers did not answer scientific inquiries with integrity or sincerity. Instead they answered with contradictions and personal complaints.
19. Supporting and encouraging the ostracization of the Complainant was considered continued harassment and discriminatory behavior against the Complainant.
20. Non-constructive interference with the Complainant's performance of his job duties was unprofessional, not useful, and unethical.

Interrogatory No. 8: State the name, address, and telephone number of each person to whom you have made any statement or statements in any form, written, oral, typed, or by electronic transmission regarding the allegations in your appeal.

OBJECTIONS: Complainant contends that all statements regarding the allegations in his current EEO case made with his attorney are privileged. In addition, the Complainant contends that all statements regarding the allegations in his current EEO case made with his parents are immaterial to the proceedings. Complainant reiterates and restates each Objection from above, and adds that this Interrogatory requests information subject to privilege, including attorney work product. Further, the incidents are so numerous that it is impossible to name them all; the main non-privileged ones are related here, but Complainant reserves the right to supplement this (and every other) Response. Without waiving any privilege, Complainant responds as follows:

RESPONSE: Complainant contends that he made statements regarding the allegations in his current EEO case with the following persons:

Name	Location/Address	Telephone
Dana Sweater		
Mr. & Mrs. Robert Sweater		
Michael J. Snider, Esq.	Snider & Associates, LLC 104 Church Lane, Suite 201 Baltimore, MD 21208	410-653-9060

Interrogatory No. 9: Provide the date of each statement, the form of each statement, whether written, oral, or by recording device, and the name, address, and telephone number of each person having possession of statements identified in Interrogatory No. 8 above, and provide a detailed summary of each oral statement;

OBJECTIONS: Complainant hereby OBJECTS to the Agency's Discovery on the grounds that said Discovery is overbroad, overly burdensome, and requests irrelevant, immaterial or inadmissible information or information protected by privilege, and/or contains multipart questions in violation of law, rule or regulation.

Complainant contends that all statements regarding the allegations in his current EEO case made with his attorney are privileged. In addition, the Complainant contends that all statements regarding the allegations in his current EEO case made with his parents are immaterial to the proceedings.

Complainant reiterates and restates each Objection from above, and adds that this Interrogatory requests information subject to privilege, including attorney work product. Further, the incidents are so numerous that it is impossible to name them all; the main ones are related here, but Complainant reserves the right to supplement this (and every other) Response. Without waiving any privilege, Complainant responds as follows:

RESPONSE: Complainant contends that he made the following statements regarding the allegations in his current EEO case with the following persons:

1.   Dana Sweater
   a.   Oral statements made at home from January 2001-present.
      i.   The Complainant told his wife that his managers were not treating him well in comparison to others (non-Jews) and that he had filed formal EEO grievances against the Agency.
      ii.   The Complainant said (as his wife was well aware from years earlier) that there was a pattern and practice of anti-Semitism in the BE Division and that he was looking to get a re-assignment to a better research group,
      iii. The Complainant told his wife that his supervisors (P. and D.) were giving the Complainant undue hardships in obtaining an alternate work schedule.
      iv.   The Complainant told his wife that his supervisors (P. and J.) were giving the Complainant undue hardships in obtaining a re-assignment out of Division to a more productive and less hostile work environment.
      v.   The Complainant told his wife that that his supervisors (P. and J.) were giving the Complainant lower than deserved ratings.
      vi.   The Complainant told his wife that his supervisor (P.) was giving the Complainant undue hardships in publishing.
      vii. The Complainant told his wife that the EEOCCRA had rejected his claim of non-compliance of his negotiated settlement agreement.
      viii. The Complainant told his wife that the ARL EEO office was inept at scheduling his mediation for which the negotiator would have the authority to approve all settlement options, like re-assignment out of Division.

Interrogatory No. 10: State whether you, your attorneys, or anyone acting on your behalf obtained statements in any form from any person regarding any of the facts alleged in your appeal. If so state the name, address, and telephone number of each person from whom any such statement was taken, the date on which each such statement was taken, the name(s) and address of the person(s) who took such statements, name(s) and address of the person(s) having custody of such statements, whether such statements were taken by writing, by recording device, by court reporter or stenographer, and provide a detailed summary of each oral statement.

OBJECTIONS: Complainant hereby OBJECTS to the Agency's Discovery on the grounds that said Discovery is overbroad, vague, overly burdensome, requests irrelevant, immaterial or inadmissible information or information protected by privilege, and/or contains multipart questions in violation of law, rule or regulation. Complainant reiterates and restates each Objection from above, and adds that this Interrogatory requests information subject to privilege, including attorney work product. Further, the incidents are so numerous that it is impossible to name them all; the main ones are related here, but Complainant reserves the right to supplement this (and every other) Response. Without waiving any privilege, Complainant responds as follows:

RESPONSE: Complainant contends that he obtained statements regarding the facts alleged in this EEO case from the following persons:

See prior response.

Interrogatory No. 11: With respect to each expert witness you intend to call at the hearing (if you intend to call any experts) state the expert's name and address, the area of his or her expertise, the subject matter on which each such expert is expected to testify, the substance of the facts and opinions to which each expert is expected to testify, and provide a summary of the grounds for each opinion of each such expert;

OBJECTIONS: Same as above.

RESPONSE: Complainant has not determined whether or not to call any expert witnesses at this time; if a determination is so made, this Interrogatory Response will be supplemented.

Interrogatory No. 12: If you are claiming any physical or emotional harm, to include stress, as a result of any action or failure to act by a government employee, state the name, business address, and business telephone number of each physician, psychologist, psychiatrist, or other medical practitioner you consulted during the period beginning January 1, 2000 and continuing to the present date.

OBJECTIONS: Complainant asserts and does not waive any doctor-patient privilege and explicitly directs the Agency to not contact any of his medical practitioners for any reason whatsoever connected with this case.

RESPONSE: Complainant consulted the following medical practitioners during the period beginning January 1, 2000 and continuing to the present date because of physical or emotional harm, to include stress, as a result of repeated actions and failures to act by multiple government employees.

Dr. A
Dr. B
C, LCSW-C
Dr. D

Interrogatory No. 13: For each such medical practitioner identified in Interrogatory 11, summarize the treatment and instructions you received from each practitioner.

OBJECTIONS: Complainant reiterates and restates each Objection from above, and adds that this Interrogatory requests information subject to privilege, including attorney work product.

Complainant reserves the right to supplement this (and every other) Response. Without waiving any privilege, Complainant responds as follows:

RESPONSE: Complainant contends that the following is a summary of the treatment and instructions received from each practitioner identified in Interrogatory No. 11.

Dr. A	Prescribes medication to help alleviate symptoms aggravated by anxiety and stress. Provides medication management counseling. Prescribes medication to help alleviate sleeplessness.
Dr. B	Requires 3-5 month return visits for medical exams. Checks weight, heart, lungs, blood pressure, etc. Takes blood samples for cholesterol screening. Provides medication management counseling.
CLCSW-C	Provided stress and anxiety management counseling. Provided counseling on maintaining and improving productivity in a hostile workplace environment.
D	Prescribed medication to help alleviate symptoms aggravated by anxiety and stress. Provided medication management counseling.

Interrogatory No. 14: Identify any diary, calendar, or other document in or on which you recorded your activities during the period beginning in January 1, 2000 and ending December 31, 2004.

OBJECTIONS: See Standard Objections, above.

RESPONSE: Complainant contends that the following is a list of documents recording his activities during the period January 1, 2000 through December 31, 2004.

1. Chronology (1 file)
2. Time record (1 file)
3. Meeting notes (notepads)
4. Lab notes (multiple files)

Interrogatory No. 15: Identify by name, position, grade, and religion each employee you allege was treated more favorably than you from January 1, 2000 to the present.

OBJECTIONS: Complainant reiterates and restates each Objection from above, and adds that this Interrogatory requests information subject to privilege, including attorney work product. Further, the incidents are so numerous that it is impossible to name them all; the main ones are related here, but Complainant reserves the right to supplement this (and every other) Response. Without waiving any privilege, Complainant responds as follows:

RESPONSE: Complainant contends that the following is a list of Division employees that **WERE NOT** treated more favorably than the Complainant from January 1, 2000 to the present.

1. A
2. B
3. C
4. D

The Complainant contends that **ALL** other Division employees and managers **WERE** treated more favorably than the Complainant (in one or more ways) from January 1, 2000 to the present.

Interrogatory No. 16: State precisely how each employee identified in Interrogatory 15 was treated more favorably than you.

OBJECTIONS: Complainant reiterates and restates each Objection from above, and adds that this Interrogatory requests information subject to privilege, including attorney work product. Further, the incidents are so numerous that it is impossible to name them all; the main ones are related here, but Complainant reserves the right to supplement this (and every other) Response. Without waiving any privilege, Complainant responds as follows:

RESPONSE: The Complainant contends that each employee and manager in the Division **other than those specifically identified** in Interrogatory No. 15 was treated more favorably in one or more of the following manners:

1. Received higher performance ratings
2. Endured fewer (if any) hardships in publishing
3. Endured fewer (if any) hardships in requesting or obtaining leave
4. Endured fewer (if any) hardships in requesting or obtaining software
5. Endured fewer (if any) hardships in spending their customer funds to support their mission research objectives
6. Endured less stringent work monitoring
7. Endured less abuse, badgering, and false allegations regarding the quality, quantity, and value of their work.
8. Endured less abuse of their intellectual property rights.
9. Received more credit for actual achievements and accomplishments
10. Received more credit for interactions with other scientists within and outside the Laboratory.
11. Received more support from management for interactions with other scientists within and outside the Laboratory.
12. Received awards
13. Received more timely responses from their managers to address work place and job-related concerns.

14. Received more timely processing of Forms.
15. Endured fewer (if any) allegations of improper timekeeping or job performance
16. Endured fewer (if any) ethnic slurs or religious based discriminations
17. Endured fewer (if any) reprisals or retaliations due to prior EEO activity or EEO related complaints.
18. Were included in Division/Branch/ Team discussions, particularly regarding topics related to their scientific area of interest.
19. Were included in Division/Branch/ Team technical manuscript or contract proposal reviews, particularly regarding topics related to their scientific area of interest.
20. Maintained (in general) higher morale and esprit de corps

Interrogatory No. 17: Identify each request you made for an adjusted work schedule from January 1, 2000 through December 31, 2004. By identify I mean give the date of the request, the form of the request (oral, written, e-mail), to whom it was made, and the specific remedy requested.

OBJECTIONS: Complainant reiterates and restates each Objection from above, and adds that this Interrogatory requests information subject to privilege, including attorney work product. Further, the incidents are so numerous that it is impossible to name them all; the main ones are related here, but Complainant reserves the right to supplement this (and every other) Response. Without waiving any privilege, Complainant responds as follows:

RESPONSE: The Complainant contends that the following is a list of his requests for an adjusted work schedule from January 1, 2000 through December 31, 2004:

1. 30 August 2001, e-mail to P

   The Complainant requested to arrive at work at 1130 Sunday through Friday.

2. 21 July 2003, e-mail to C

   The Complainant requested to arrive at work at 1115 Monday through Friday and no later than 1500 on Sunday.

3. 21 July 2003, e-mail to D

   The Complainant requested to work from 1115-1945 Monday through Thursday, 1115-1515 Friday and 1515-1915 on Sunday.

4. 24 July 2003, e-mail to P

   The Complainant requested to work from 1115-1945 Monday through Thursday,

1115-1515 Friday, and 1515-1915 on Sunday.

Interrogatory No. 18: Describe the response received to each request identified in response to Interrogatory No: 17.

OBJECTIONS: Complainant reiterates and restates each Objection from above, and adds that this Interrogatory requests information subject to privilege, including attorney work product. Further, the incidents are so numerous that it is impossible to name them all; the main ones are related here, but Complainant reserves the right to supplement this (and every other) Response. Without waiving any privilege, Complainant responds as follows:

RESPONSE: The Complainant contends that the following list describes the responses received to his requests for an adjusted work schedule identified in Interrogatory No. 17:

1.   "No"

Interrogatory No. 19: Please identify any physical limitations that impact your ability to care for your children. By identify, I mean give the medical diagnosis and impact of physical limitations on such activities as preparation of food, dressing and/or bathing children, operation of a motor vehicle, and similar activities.

OBJECTIONS: Complainant hereby OBJECTS to the Agency's Discovery on the grounds that said Discovery is overbroad, overly burdensome, and requests irrelevant, immaterial or inadmissible information or information protected by privilege, and/or contains multipart questions in violation of law, rule or regulation. Complainant reiterates and restates each Objection from above, and adds that this Interrogatory requests information subject to privilege, including attorney work product. Further, the facts are so numerous that it is impossible to name them all; the main ones are related here, but Complainant reserves the right to supplement this (and every other) Response. Without waiving any privilege, Complainant responds as follows:

RESPONSE: The Complainant contends that the following list describes the physical limitations that impact his ability to care for children:

1.   chronic pain condition in lower extremities and lower back that resulted from two previous injuries.
2.   disabled because of this chronic pain.
3.   irreversible and agonizing nerve damage and unhealed, overly sensitive scar tissue in her right knee and left foot.
4.   medical treatment 1-2 times per week.

Interrogatory No. 20: Is your wife employed outside the home? By employed I mean does she engage in activities that produce an income and/or engage in volunteer activities for non-profit organizations.

OBJECTIONS: Relevance, privilege.

Interrogatory No. 21: If your response to Interrogatory No. 20 is yes, give the name address and telephone number or her employer or the volunteer organization for which she works.

OBJECTIONS: Same as above.

Interrogatory No. 22: Describe in detail how your children are transported to and from school each day.

OBJECTIONS: Complainant hereby OBJECTS to the Agency's Discovery on the grounds that said Discovery requests irrelevant, immaterial or inadmissible information or information protected by privilege.

Interrogatory No. 23: Identify the place where you perform morning prayers. By identify I mean give the place name, address, and telephone number.

OBJECTIONS: Complainant reiterates and restates each Objection from above, and adds that this Interrogatory requests information subject to privilege, including attorney work product. Objection based upon relevance. Further, the information is so numerous that it is impossible to name them all; the main ones are related here, but Complainant reserves the right to supplement this (and every other) Response. Without waiving any privilege, Complainant responds as follows:

RESPONSE: The Complainant contends that he conducts weekday morning prayers at work in his office.

The Complainant contends that he conducts silent (or quiet) meditation and prayer in his office (most often from 1100-1145 and later at or close to sunset for approx. 10 minutes) at work to meet daily religious obligations.

The Complainant contends that this activity is done on his own time (as one who engages in physical exercise activities) and does not in any way affect his scientific productivity or cause any hardship to the normal business of the Agency.

The Complainant contends that only occasionally he conducts weekday morning prayers from 0900-1030 AM Synagogue.

The Complainant contends that only rarely he conducts weekday morning prayers from 0630-0730 and/or from 0915-1015 AM at Synagogue #2.

Interrogatory No. 24: State the time of day that daily prayer services are available at the location identified above.

OBJECTIONS: Same as above.

RESPONSE: The Complainant contends that no daily prayer services with a quorum are available at the U.S. Navy Laboratory.

Interrogatory No. 25: Please identify the specific term of the negotiated settlement agreement you signed on 24 July 1998 you allege management attempted to coerce you to change. By identify I mean give the page, paragraph, and line of the agreement management wanted to change.

OBJECTIONS: Confidential.

Interrogatory No. 26: State precisely how management wanted to change the term of the agreement identified in Interrogatory No. 25 above.

OBJECTIONS: Confidential.

Respectfully Submitted,

_____
Michael J. Snider, Esq.
Law Offices of Snider & Associates, LLC

Appendix E

Sample Post-Hearing Brief

EQUAL EMPLOYMENT OPPORTUNITY COMMISSION
Philadelphia District Office
The Bourse, Suite 400
21 South 5th Street
Philadelphia, Pennsylvania 19106-2515

Mr. Client,	)
	)
	)
COMPLAINANT,	)
vs.	)
	)
COMMISSIONER, ******	)
ADMINISTRATION,	)
	)
AGENCY.	)
	)

COMPLAINANT'S POST HEARING BRIEF

The Complainant, by and through his attorney, Michael J. Snider, Esq., hereby submits his Post Hearing Brief in this case, and states:

Introduction

Complainant believes that he has been discriminated against on the basis of his race, color, and / or sex. The Complainant was objectively *much higher qualified* than any other candidate in his area, and was clearly *much higher qualified* than many of the other selectees outside of his protected classes. The Agency destroyed essential information in this case and failed to present non-discriminatory reasons for its actions in this case sufficiently specific to allow the Complainant a reasonable opportunity for rebuttal. Complainant hereby incorporates his **Pre-Hearing Statement** and all other pleadings by reference.

Standard and Burden of Proof

Discrimination cases generally turn on circumstantial evidence. **Gavalik v. Continental Can**

Co., 812 F.2d 834, 852 (3d Cir. 1987), **cert. denied**, 484 U.S. 979 (1987). A presumption of discrimination arises when a prima facie case is established. **McDonnell-Douglas Corp. v. Green**, 411 U.S. 792 (1973); **Texas Dep't of Community Affairs v. Burdine**, 450 U.S. 248 (1981). Initially, it is the burden of the complainant to establish that there is some substance to her allegation of discrimination. In order to sustain this burden, the complainant must establish a prima facie case of discrimination. **McDonnell Douglas Corp**; **Furnco Construction Co. v. Waters**, 438 U.S. 567 (1978). This means that the complainant must present a body of evidence such that, were it not rebutted, the trier of fact *could conclude that unlawful discrimination did occur.*

In the present case Complainant can establish a **prima facie** case of color, race or gender discrimination by showing:

(1) he was a member of a protected class or classes;

(2) he was qualified for the position for which he applied;

(3) he was not recommended, hired or promoted despite his qualifications; and

(4) the job was given to a person outside of the protected group(s).

Keyes v. Secretary of the Navy, 47 FEP Cases 891, 896 (1st Cir. 1988).

St. Mary's Honor Center v. Hicks, 509 U.S. 502 (1993) held that once the plaintiff establishes a prima facie case, the defendant must then produce evidence that it took the action for a legitimate, non-discriminatory reason. If the defendant fails to meet its burden, judgment must be entered in favor of the plaintiff as a matter of law. If the defendant is able to meet its burden, the plaintiff may show that the defendant's proffered reasons are pretextual. Once the factfinder finds that the proffered reasons are pretext, it may find discrimination. **See Sheridan v. E.I. DuPont de Nemours and Co.**, 100 F.3d 1061 (3rd Cir. 1996)(en banc), **cert denied**, – U.S. –, 128 L.Ed.2d 1031 (1997). The factfinder need find only that the discriminatory or retaliatory motive was a substantial motivating factor to find that the employer is liable.

In order to prevail, Complainant must show that the agency's reasons for its actions were a pretext to mask discrimination, either because the agency *more likely* had a discriminatory motive, or because the stated reasons *lacked credibility*. **Burdine** at 248. Further, evidence of preselection operates to discredit the agency's explanation for its decision. **Goostree v. State of Tennessee**, 796 F.2d 854, 861 (6th Cir.1986).

The Commission has also held that, pursuant to **Burdine**, certain statements – due to their vague nature – *cannot, as a matter of law,* serve to form nondiscriminatory reasons for nonselection. **William Hogsten v. Shalala**, EEO No. 01A00208 (April 5, 2000).[2]

The United States Supreme Court addressed this issue explicitly, in **Texas Dept. Of Community Affairs V. Burdine, 450 U.S. 248 (1981)(emphasis added)**:

"The burden that shifts to the defendant, therefore, is to rebut the presumption of discrimination by producing evidence that the plaintiff was rejected, or someone else was preferred, for a legitimate, nondiscriminatory reason. The defendant need not persuade the court that it was actually motivated by the proffered reasons. See Sweeney, supra, at 25. It is sufficient if the defendant's evidence raises a genuine issue of fact as to whether it discriminated against the plaintiff. FN 8 [450 U.S. 248, 255] To accomplish this, the defendant must **clearly set forth**, through the introduction of admissible evidence, the reasons for the plaintiff's rejection. FN 9 The **explanation provided must be legally sufficient** to justify a judgment for the defendant. If the defendant carries this burden of production, the presumption raised by the prima facie case is rebutted, FN 10 and the factual inquiry proceeds to a new level of specificity. Placing this burden of production on the defendant thus serves simultaneously to meet the plaintiff's prima facie case by presenting a legitimate reason for the action and to **frame the factual issue with sufficient clarity so that the [450 U.S. 248, 256] plaintiff will have a *full and fair opportunity to demonstrate pretext*.** The sufficiency of the defendant's evidence should be evaluated by the extent to which it fulfills these functions."

The plaintiff retains the burden of persuasion. He now **must have the opportunity to demonstrate that the proffered reason was not the true reason** for the employment decision. This burden now merges with the ultimate burden of persuading the court that she has been the victim of intentional discrimination. She may succeed in this either directly by persuading the court that a discriminatory reason more likely motivated the employer or indirectly by showing that the employer's proffered explanation is unworthy of credence. See **McDonnell Douglas**, 411 U.S., at 804 -805."

In a recent case (eerily similar to the instant matter), the EEOC OFO found discrimination on the basis of gender and race for non-selection of a white male ABC Representative to the GS-9 XYZ Specialist position. **Michael A. O'Brien v. Massanari, Commissioner, Social Security Administration**, EEOC OFO, Agency No. 9950.SSA; EEOC 07A10034, 102 FEOR 1051 (October 3, 2001)(attached).

In cases involving nonselections, a complainant may demonstrate that the agency's reason for its action was a pretext for discrimination by showing that he was better qualified or "plainly superior" to the selectee, but still was not selected. **See Patterson v. McLean Credit Union**, 491 U.S. 164, 187-88 (1989); **Isadore v. Dep't of the Interior**, EEOC Request No. 05930335 (September 23, 1993).

Argument

The Complainant Has Proven A Prima Facie Case of Discrimination, Which – If Left Unrebutted – Entitles Him To Prevail in this Matter

The Complainant has proven a **prima facie** case of discrimination. He is a male, and is Caucasian. One Selectee from the same component, Ms. Selectee (black, female) is not in his protected classes. Other Selectees for the position, including A, B and C, were female, black or both. The Complainant was qualified for the position and was not recommended or promoted, being ranked *27th out of 27* candidates in his component.

As stated above, once the Complainant establishes a **prima facie** case, the Agency must then produce evidence that it took the action for a legitimate, non-discriminatory reason. If the defendant fails to meet its burden, judgment must be entered in favor of the plaintiff as a matter of law. **St. Mary's Honor Center v. Hicks**, 509 U.S. 502 (1993).

An Adverse Inference Should Be Drawn From the Agency's Failure to Preserve Evidence

The Agency did not address its failure to preserve evidence in this case. "The blackboard was erased," confirmed each of the management witnesses. The ranking process that was not recorded, or was recorded and then erased in violation of the law, would have shown that the Complainant would have been selected but for intentional discrimination. The Agency's complete failure to even offer an excuse as to this destruction of evidence is concerning at the least. **See** Rule 37(b)(2)(A) of the Federal Rules of Civil Procedure.

The United States Supreme Court has sanctioned the use of the "adverse inference rule," namely, that if the information had been provided, it would have been unfavorable to the agency and favorable to the opposing party. **See Insurance Corp. of Ireland v. Compayne Des Bauxites**, 456 U.S. 694, 705 (1982), **Hammond Packing Co. v. Arkansas**, 212 U.S. 322, 350-1 (1909). As in the attached EEOC decision, these "records destroyed by the agency were highly relevant to the matters raised" in this Complaint. Further, "The agency's failure to make any effort to reconstruct the record is evidence of bad faith." **Reginald T. Huey v. Department of Health and Human Services Equal Employment Opportunity Commission, EEOC** 01831403, 86 FEOR 3088 (February 28, 1986).

The Agency Failed To Present A Legitimate, Non-Discriminatory Reason For Non-Selection of the Complainant Sufficiently Specific To Allow Meaningful Rebuttal

The Agency attempted to explain its selection of Ms. Selectee, but was unsuccessful. It simply did not proffer reasons with sufficient specificity to allow Complainant an opportunity to offer meaningful rebuttal. The Agency used "fuzzy" subjective criteria that were impossible to quantify. "...subjective criteria are particularly easy for an employer to invent in an effort to sabotage a plaintiff's prima facie case and mask discrimination." **McDonald v. Eastern Wyoming Mental Health Ctr.**, 941 F.2d 1115 (1991). Further, the Commission has noted that when a Complainant's qualifications are objectively better than the Selectee's, an **extremely heavy burden** is imposed upon the Agency to justify its actions with proof that the selection was *based upon **proper** subjective considerations*. **Long v. NASA**, EEOC Appeal No. 01941238 (September 8, 1994), **citing Adams v. Gaudet**, 515 F.Supp. 1086 (W.D. La. 1981).. When the record indicates that a Complainant is objectively more qualified than Selectee, the Commission will *closely scrutinize* the Agency's proffered subjective basis for selecting the Selectee over Complainant. **Joseph T. Varley v. Reno, Attorney General, Department of Justice**, EEOC 01972338, 99 FEOR 1072 (December 3, 1998). See **Young v. Treasury**, EEOC No. 01933006 (March 9, 1994); **Miles v. M.N.C. Corp.**, 750 F.2d 867, 871 (1985).

It is well established that pretext can be shown when the Complainant is qualified to perform a position at a higher grade level than the Selectee and the Selection is based on different assumptions about the respective qualities of the candidates without a solid factual basis for making the assumptions. **Byler v. Secretary of the Air Force**, EEOC 01923010 (1993). Here, Complainant had many years of service not only at the GS-12 grade level, but actually making adjudicatory claims decisions (for an Administrative Law Judge) – precisely the type of work required by the position in question.

The Commission has held that subjective determinations, in particular, require that the Agency produce solid evidence to substantiate its position. Failure to do so exposes the Agency to the risk that the Complainant will take advantage of the Agency's lack of proof to establish pretext. **Weaver v. USPS**, 01860291 (1987). In particular, when subjective determinations make up the Agency's legitimate reason, the Agency must present more evidence than just the conclusory testimony of the selecting official. In **Parker v. Postmaster General**, EEOC 05900110 (1990), the Selecting Official did not cite sufficient examples to illustrate his conclusions. The Commission accordingly found that the Agency failed to sustain its burden of production because the issue was not sufficiently framed for pretext by such conclusory testimony, stating that "Where a candidate is found to be objectively better qualified than the selectee, the use of subjective criteria such as **aggressiveness, initiative, and leadership potential**, while not impermissible, may offer a convenient pretext for giving force and effect to racial prejudice, especially in this case where the subjective reasons given for not choosing appellant were unsupported by any independent evidence." **Parker**, supra (**emphasis added**). Further, an Agency cannot simply hide behind its own stated policies, without explaining how those policies apply in a particular case. In the absence of a suitable explanation, the Agency fails to meet its burden of production. **Jones v. Postmaster General**, 01950129 (1996).

Higher education degrees can add to a candidate's qualifications in much the same way as extensive work experience. **Currie v. Dept of the Navy**, EEOC 01831303 (1987). The Complainant's advanced degree in this case made him clearly the most qualified.

The Agency notably failed entirely to present any legitimate non-discriminatory reasons for its selection of the other individuals identified by the Complainant, including (for example and not by way of limitation) A, B or C. This total failure to present evidence should be taken as an adverse inference. Further, the inconsistencies in testimony of Agency managers is indicative of pretext. Pretext is often demonstrated by showing the record of the Agency's actions contains "inconsistencies" and discrepancies that render the Agency's proffered explanations unworthy of credence. **Williams v. Dept of the Army**, 01842729 (1986).

The Agency's Witnesses Were Not Credible

The Agency's witnesses contradicted themselves and each other in this case. Since a transcript was not available at the time of writing of this brief, Complainant is unable to point to exact pages in which the contradictions were found, but believes that it was made clear at the hearing which statements were contradictory. The Agency witnesses were unable to explain how the rankings were developed, and no evidence was introduced regarding that method. In similar cases, the Commission has found that Agencies *fail to meet their burden*. See, e.g., **Jones vs.**

Postmaster General, EEOC 01950129 (1996).

In the Alternative, Complainant Presented a Complete Rebuttal of the Agency's Proffered Non-Discriminatory Reasons for Non-Selection

In this case, the Complainant has presented evidence which tends to demonstrate that his qualifications were superior to those of the selectees and the other recommended candidates. **See Bauer v. Bailer**, 647 F.2d 1037, 1048 (10th Cir. 1981); **Guyton v. Department of Veterans Affairs**, EEOC Appeal No. 01931099 (December 7, 1993). Mr. Complainant was by far objectively the best candidate for the position, and would have been selected **but for** the Agency's discrimination against him. He should have been selected for promotion based on his work experience, professional qualifications and educational background. He met and exceeded the work experience criteria described in the vacancy announcement, the selection factors, and the position description. Mr. Complainant's career accomplishments were superior to that of the Selectees.

Complainant attended the ABC University School of Law and was admitted to the AA State Bar in October. He has practiced law continuously since that time. The Agency knew or should have known all of this information.

The Complainant spent years as a GS-12 Attorney Advisor writing opinions for a X Administration Administrative Law Judge. He also spent two years as a GS-9 and then GS-11 Attorney Advisor writing opinions for a X Administration Administrative Law Judge. He wrote over 1000 opinions and always had sterling performance evaluations.

He also spent 4 years in the Asset Claims Division of the Resolution Trust Corporation under the Federal Deposit Insurance Corporation reviewing and resolving **claims** for assets sold under contractual arrangements. Two of those years were as a GS-12 Senior Claims Analyst in the Real Estate Section, Sales Section, and Financial Instruments Division, and then two years as a GS-12 Senior Claims Analyst.

Further, as noted above, the Agency has failed to state sufficiently specific reasons for the Complainant's non-selection, and has therefore failed to rebut the Complainant's **prima facie** case of discrimination. Even the Agency's proffered reasons, however, fall short. The Agency has not, and can not, explain why Mr. Complainant was not selected. The Agency's proffered reasons were rebutted completely. The Agency's witnesses contradicted themselves and each other.

Officials involved in the hiring process s stated that although there was a discussion and rating/ranking of candidates, *no written information was saved*. The Complainant was *never interviewed*. His oral skills were *never evaluated objectively*. His details were ignored, but others were considered. His past experience was not considered, but that of others was considered. Worst of all, no notes were preserved from the "closed door" meeting, and the "blackboard was erased."

Higher rankings in the Complainants' component were given to Female, Black and/or Hispanic candidates, who had **negative comments** on their written narrative evaluations where the Complainant had *no negative comments*.   This is probative of discriminatory intent on the part of the black supervisors who controlled the process.

One must keep in mind that **not one of the applicants for the position of Claims Authorizer involved herein knows how to do the job.**   Each person selected must complete a nine month training course successfully.   Experience representative of being able to perform the job is certainly therefore contemplated by the recommended Guidance statement, and the only one with that experience was the Complainant.

Finally, it was clear from the Complainant's credible testimony and demeanor at the hearing that his oral skills, analytical ability and technical prowess are clearly exceptional.   This strongly mitigates against the Agency's unsupported and subjective assessments of the Complainant and instead is suggestive of intentional discrimination.

Documentary Evidence Supports Complainant's Contentions of Discrimination

The Complainant also showed that the Agency discriminated against him on the basis of his gender and/or race when it failed to comply with the provisions of the National Agreement between the American Federation of Government Employees and the X Administration (CX 9)("National Agreement").   The National Agreement clearly states that where an underrepresentation exists, management must give "serious consideration" to applicants from the underrepresented groups for a targeted occupation (CX 9 at Article 26, Section 11 (C), page 142).   Further, the Agency agreed that:

"Should adverse EEO impact be evidenced pursuant to the Affirmative Employment Program Plan, specific and measurable objectives shall be set to correct the conditions.   Those objectives will include but not be limited to:

A. Validating existing selection procedures or;

B. Modifying or substituting selection procedures to alleviate adverse impact."

(CX 9 at Article 18, Section 3, page 100).

Complainant's Exhibit C-7 clearly showed a manifest imbalance of white males at the relevant grade levels.   This systemic evidence of adverse impact on his protected class(es) is probative of the Agency's discrimination in this case, especially given the Agency's failure to act on the imbalance or change in any way the selection process to alleviate the imbalance.   Further, it failed to give "serious consideration," or any different consideration, to white males despite a clear obligation to do so.

Conclusion

The Complainant was discriminated against on the basis of his gender and/or race and/or color. He requests only that he be made whole.

Respectfully Submitted,

Date: _____   _____

                                   Michael J. Snider, Esq.
                                   Attorney for Complainant

Appendix F

Sample Notice of Appeal

**NOTICE OF APPEAL/PETITION
TO THE EQUAL EMPLOYMENT OPPORTUNITY COMMISSION**

OFFICE OF FEDERAL OPERATIONS
P.O. Box 19848
Washington, DC 20036

Complainant Information: (Please Print or Type)

Complainant's name (Last, First, M.I.):	
Home/mailing address:	
City, State, ZIP Code:	
Daytime Telephone # (with area code):	
E-mail address (if any):	

Attorney/Representative Information (if any):

Attorney name:	
Non-Attorney Representative name:	
Address:	
City, State, ZIP Code:	
Telephone number (if applicable):	
E-mail address (if any):	

General Information:

Name of the agency being charged with discrimination:	
Identify the Agency's complaint number:	
Location of the duty station or local facility in which the complaint arose:	

Has a **final action** been taken by the agency, an Arbitrator, FLRA, or MSPB on this complaint?	_____Yes; Date Received _____(Remember to attach a copy) _____No _____This appeal alleges a breach of settlement agreement
Has a complaint been filed on this same matter with the EEOC, <u>another</u> agency, or through any <u>other</u> administrative or collective bargaining procedures?	_____No _____Yes (Indicate the agency or procedure, complaint/docket number, and attach a copy, if appropriate)
Has a civil action (lawsuit) been filed in connection with this complaint?	_____No _____Yes **(Attach a copy of the civil action filed)**

NOTICE: Please **attach a copy of the final decision or order** from which you are appealing. If a hearing was requested, please attach a copy of the agency's final order and a copy of the EEOC Administrative Judge's decision. Any comments or brief in support of this appeal MUST be filed with the EEOC **and** with the agency **within 30 days** of the date this appeal is filed. The date the appeal is filed is the date on which it is postmarked, hand delivered, or faxed to the EEOC at the address above.

Signature of complainant or complainant's representative:	
Date:	

Then simply mail this form to:

Equal Employment Opportunity Commission
Office of Federal Operations
P. O. Box 19848
Washington, D.C. 20036

Alternatively, you can hand-deliver your appeal to:

Equal Employment Opportunity Commission
Office of Federal Operations
1801 L Street, N.W.
Washington, D.C. 20507

Appendix G

Recommended Reading List

1. **A Guide to Federal Sector Equal Employment Law and Practice** by Ernest C. Hadley, Dewey Publications. http://www.deweypub.com/

2. **Assessing Compensatory Damages Claims in Federal EEO Cases — Second Edition** By Lucinda A. Riley, Esq., and Allison Uehling, Esq, LRP Publications. http://www.shoplrp.com/federal/cat-EEO.html

3. **Compensatory Damages and Other Remedies in Federal Sector Employment Discrimination Cases, Second Edition, 2003 plus 2005 Supplement**, By Gary M. Gilbert, Dewey Publications. http://www.deweypub.com/

4. **EEO Discovery Forms Book For Agency Representatives Interrogatories, Document Requests, Definitions, Instrictions,** By Ernest C. Hadley and Renn C. Fowler. http://www.deweypub.com/

5. **Frequently Asked Questions About The Federal Sector Hearing Process,** http://www.eeoc.gov/federal/faq_fshp.html

Index